MasterChef
1997

MasterChef 1997

Foreword by Loyd Grossman

General Editor: Janet Illsley

EBURY PRESS
LONDON

First published 1997

1 3 5 7 9 10 8 6 4 2

First published in the United Kingdom in 1997 by Ebury Press,
Random House, 20 Vauxhall Bridge Road, London SW1V 2SA

Random House Australia (Pty) Limited
20 Alfred Street, Milsons Point, Sydney,
New South Wales 2061, Australia

Random House New Zealand Limited
18 Poland Road, Glenfield
Auckland 10, New Zealand

Random House South Africa (Pty) Limited
Endulini, 5A Jubilee Road, Parktown 2193, South Africa

Random House UK Limited Reg. No. 954009

A CIP catalogue record for this book is available from the British Library

ISBN: 0 09 185305 2

MasterChef 1997
A Union Pictures production for BBC North

Series devised by Franc Roddam
Executive Producers: Bradley Adams and Richard Kalms
Producer and Director: Richard Bryan
Associate Producer: Glynis Robertson
Production Co-ordinators: Julia Park and Katy Savage

General Editor: Janet Illsley
Design: Clive Dorman

Typeset in Garamond by Clive Dorman & Co.
Printed and bound in Great Britain by Mackays of Chatham plc, Kent.

Papers used by Ebury Press are natural recyclable products made from wood
grown in sustainable forests.

Contents

Cookery Notes

- All recipes serve 4, unless otherwise indicated.
- Both metric and imperial measures are given for the recipes. Follow one set of measurements only, not a combination, because they are not interchangeable.
- All spoon measures are level unless otherwise stated.
- Ovens must be preheated to the specified temperature. Grills should also be preheated.
- Size 2 eggs should be used except where otherwise specified. Free-range eggs are recommended.
- Use fresh herbs unless otherwise suggested.
- Stocks should be freshly made if possible. Alternatively buy good quality ready-made stock.
- If you do not have an ice-cream maker, freeze ice cream in a shallow container, whisking several times during freezing to ensure an even-textured result.

Foreword

More accurately than most market research, MasterChef reflects which ingredients and flavours are exciting British cooks at the moment. Some of the menus of the early 90's showed the sort of elaboration that isn't often found outside restaurant dishes, but increasingly our contestants have cast their nets more widely combining old family favourites with tastes and techniques picked up on holidays abroad, or using ideas and ingredients from today's leading professional chefs. Earthy, hearty flavours have cropped up in many of this year's dishes. Wild mushrooms (some a bit tamer than others) have been all over the shop and pork and duck have frequently been paired with rich dark sauces often made with a surprising variety of arcane country wines. Lamb has been the dominant meat this year and our judges were consistently impressed by the rich and delicious varieties of British lamb that our cooks chose. Indeed throughout the competition there has been an assiduous search for the best ingredients on the market. Our contestants have certainly made use of the encyclopaedic larders of the British supermarkets, but they have also sought out small, specialist suppliers. More than ever before the best cooks are also the most demanding shoppers.

Homely ingredients were very much in the ascendancy this year with many of our contestants showing a new found fascination for root vegetables. Parsnips, potatoes and swede were all popular. Our cooks were also fond of celeriac and fennel, and cabbage was treated with newfound respect. More menus than ever were fishy this year. Whilst some of them featured second mortgage fish like sea bass or dover sole it was good to see creative dishes with the more affordable smoked haddock. Professional chefs are increasingly influenced by Japanese and South-east Asian cooking and these influences popped up here and there on our menus too – as many of our cooks have have been enticed by Thai flavours in particular. As always puddings were irreproachable – this is Britain after all – although this year they were being cooked with a lighter touch and many of our judges remarked how uncloying even the richer looking puddings were.

There are a few outstanding questions. Why don't we have vegetarian menus? How about more cooking that derives from different cultures within Britain? Will beef make a comeback? Only next year's contestants can provide the answers.

Loyd Grossman

Introduction

If someone had told me in 1990, as I entered the studio to direct the first series of MasterChef, that seven years and more than 150 programmes later I would be writing this introduction, I would certainly have laughed. Not that I have lacked faith in the competition at any time, but I would never have imagined that year after year it would continue to enthrall me as it does. The reason, though, is very clear. The whole competition, for the crew, the judges and especially the contestants is enormous fun.

Not that it isn't hard work: several of the twenty-seven cooks who come to know the red, yellow and blue kitchens are persuaded to take part by their friends or family. When they win through in the preliminary 'cook-offs' held at catering colleges around Britain, contestants suddenly find themselves eating, talking and dreaming menus, herbs and spices, with everything else in their lives being relegated to the back burner. Many a family has vowed they will never again eat the dishes endlessly practised.

It has always been our aim to keep the studio atmosphere as relaxed as possible. Most of the food loving crew have been with MasterChef for many years, and carry a full set of cutlery in the back pocket for all eventualities. Even the six washer-uppers, who struggle with the huge piles of plates and pans twice a day, are regulars and wouldn't miss it for the world.

So if you have ever felt that you might like to take part, we can promise you that, however far you get in the competition, you will have a lot of fun. Post a large stamped addressed envelope to:

MasterChef, PO Box 359, Kerdiston, Norwich NR10 4UU

and we will send you an application form for MasterChef 1998 together with everything you need to know about the competition. And maybe next year you will be joining us on the big bread board!

Richard Bryan

Soups
& Starters

Pumpkin Soup

25 g (1 oz) butter
30 ml (2 tbsp) olive oil
125 g (4 oz) best-quality smoked bacon,
  derinded and finely chopped
1 onion, finely chopped
1 large potato, peeled and chopped
1 carrot, peeled and chopped
700 g (1½ lb) peeled, seeded butternut
  squash or orange-fleshed pumpkin, roughly
  chopped
2.5 ml (½ tsp) chopped marjoram
750 ml (1½ pints) chicken stock
dash of Tabasco sauce
pinch of freshly grated nutmeg
salt and freshly ground black pepper
250 ml (8 fl oz) double cream

To Serve:
Rosemary and Pine Nut Bread (see right)

1 Melt the butter in a large pan with the olive oil. Add the bacon and onion and fry until soft and beginning to turn brown. Add the chopped potato, carrot, squash or pumpkin and marjoram; cook for a further 5 minutes.

2 Add the stock, Tabasco, nutmeg and seasoning. Simmer, covered, for 15-20 minutes until all the vegetables are soft.

3 Remove from the heat and let cool slightly, then purée in a food processor or blender, in batches if necessary. To ensure a smooth-textured result, pass the soup through a sieve into a clean pan.

4 Add the cream and check the seasoning. Reheat gently but do not allow to boil. Ladle into warmed soup bowls and serve with the warm bread.

Rosemary and Pine Nut Bread

15 g (½ oz) dried yeast (see note)
300 ml (½ pint) warm water
pinch of sugar
450 g (1 lb) strong plain (bread) flour
2.5 ml (½ tsp) salt
15 ml (1 tbsp) chopped rosemary
60 ml (2 fl oz) olive oil
50 g (2 oz) pine nuts

1 Blend the yeast with the water and sugar and leave for 10 minutes, until frothy.

2 Put the flour, salt and rosemary into a large bowl and make a well in the centre. Add the yeast mixture and three quarters of the olive oil. Mix to a soft dough.

3 Turn onto a lightly floured surface and knead for 5 minutes, then add the pine nuts and knead for a further 2 minutes. (To help incorporate the nuts you may require a little extra flour.)

4 Place the dough in an oiled bowl, cover with a damp cloth and leave to rise in a warm place for approximately 40 minutes.

5 On a lightly floured surface, knock back the dough and shape into 1 large or 2 small rounds. Place on a well oiled baking sheet and brush with the remaining olive oil. Leave to rise for a further 20 minutes.

6 Bake in a preheated oven at 220°C (425°F) mark 7 for about 40 minutes or until the bread is golden and sounds hollow when tapped underneath. Cool on a wire rack. Serve while still warm.

Note: If using easy-blend fast action dried yeast, follow the packet instructions.

Thai Prawn and Coconut Soup

850 ml (1⅓ pints) coconut milk (ie 2 cans)
4 kaffir lime leaves
2 large lemon grass stalks
1 small bunch of coriander root (washed
    thoroughly)
4 hot green chillies
5 cm (2 inch) piece fresh root ginger, peeled
    and sliced
5 cm (2 inch) piece fresh galangal root,
    peeled and sliced
6 raw King prawns
30 ml (2 tbsp) Thai fish sauce
juice of 1 lemon

To Garnish:
chives
coriander sprigs

To Serve:
Tomato Bread (see right)

1 Bring the coconut milk to the boil in a saucepan. Add the lime leaves, lemon grass, coriander root, chillies, ginger and galangal. Allow to infuse for 15 minutes over a very low heat. Strain the soup through a fine sieve and discard all flavourings.

2 Shell and de-vein the prawns, then split each one in half lengthwise.

3 Add the prawns to the soup and return to the heat. Cook until the prawns turn pink – no more than 2 minutes. Add the fish sauce and lemon juice.

4 Divide the soup between warmed soup bowls, distributing the prawns equally. Garnish with chives and coriander. Serve immediately, with the warm tomato bread.

Warm Tomato Bread

450 g (1 lb) strong plain (bread) flour
10 ml (2 tsp) salt
25 g (1 oz) fresh yeast
275 ml (9 oz) warm water
30 ml (2 tbsp) olive oil
10 ml (2 tsp) sun-dried tomato paste

1 Sift the flour and salt into a large bowl and make a well in the middle. Dissolve the yeast in the warm water, then add to the flour with the oil and mix to a smooth dough.

2 Turn onto a lightly floured surface and knead for 8 minutes until elastic. Cover and leave to rise in a warm place for 1 hour or until doubled in size.

3 Knock back the dough and add the tomato paste; knead for a further 2 minutes.

4 Flatten the dough slightly, then fold into three and place in a greased 450 g (1 lb) loaf tin. Cover with oiled cling film and leave to rise in a warm place for about 20 minutes until the dough has risen to the top of the tin.

5 Bake in a preheated oven at 200°C (400°F) mark 6 for 10 minutes then reduce the oven temperature to 180°C (350°F) mark 4 and bake for a further 20 minutes or until the loaf sounds hollow when tapped underneath. Cool on a wire rack. Serve warm.

Leek and Watercress Soup with Mussels and Lime

2 large leeks
1 celery stick
2 carrots
1 onion
¼ celeriac
15 ml (1 tbsp) light olive oil
1 kg (2¼ lb) mussels in shell
100 ml (3½ fl oz) dry vermouth
small handful of flat-leaf parsley
400 ml (14 fl oz) water
juice and finely grated zest of 1 lime, or to
    taste
3 or 4 large bunches watercress
salt and freshly ground black pepper

To Garnish:
30 ml (2 tbsp) crème fraîche
30 ml (2 tbsp) single cream
2 ripe tomatoes, skinned, deseeded and diced
few snipped chives
12 watercress leaves

1 Finely dice the leeks, celery, carrots, onion and celeriac. Heat the olive oil in a saucepan, add the diced vegetables, cover and sweat gently until softened, without browning.

2 Soak the mussels in cold water. Scrub the shells, remove the beards and discard any mussels which are open or have broken shells.

3 Place the mussels in a large pan with the vermouth, cover tightly and cook over a high heat for 3-5 minutes, shaking the pan frequently, until the shells open. Strain and reserve the cooking liquor. Discard any mussels which have not opened.

4 Add the reserved mussel liquor to the softened vegetables with the parsley, water and lime zest. Bring to a simmer, cover and cook gently for 30 minutes.

5 In the meantime, remove most of the mussels from their shells, leaving a few in shell for garnish.

6 Tip the contents of the pan into a food processor and whizz to a purée. Add the watercress and process again until smooth. Add the lime juice and seasoning to taste; adding pepper only if necessary – the watercress has a subtle pepperiness all its own.

7 Pass the soup through a fine sieve into a clean pan, pressing to extract as much liquid from the pulp as possible. Add the shelled mussels.

8 Gently reheat the soup, without letting it boil, and check the seasoning. Lightly whip the cream with the crème fraîche. Pour the soup into warmed bowls and swirl the cream on top. Garnish with the chopped tomato, reserved mussels, watercress leaves and a sprinkling of chives. Serve at once.

Mussel and Butternut Squash Soup with Toasted Pumpkin Seeds

450 g (1 lb) mussels in shells
150 ml (¼ pint) dry white wine (or fish
  stock)
3 cloves garlic, crushed
15 ml (1 tbsp) chopped parsley
50 g (2 oz) butter
1 onion, finely chopped
2.5 ml (½ tsp) ground cumin
2.5 ml (½ tsp) ground coriander
450 g (1 lb) peeled and deseeded butternut
  squash, cubed
45 ml (3 tbsp) double cream
30-45 ml (2-3 tbsp) milk (optional)

To Serve:
60 ml (4 tbsp) toasted pumpkin seeds

1 Soak the mussels in cold water. Scrub the shells, remove the beards and discard any mussels which are open and do not close when sharply tapped, and any with broken shells.

2 Place the mussels in a large pan with the wine, garlic and parsley. Cover tightly and cook until the shells are opened; this should take about 5 minutes.

3 Strain and reserve the cooking liquor. Discard any mussels which have not opened. Remove the mussels from their shells, reserving a few in shell for the garnish. Set aside.

4 Heat the butter in a large saucepan, add the onion and fry gently until softened. Stir in the cumin and coriander and cook for 1 minute. Add the cubes of butternut squash and reserved cooking liquor. Cover and simmer for 20-30 minutes until the squash is tender.

5 Remove from the heat and add half of the shelled mussels and the cream. Purée the soup in a food processor or blender until a velvety smooth texture is achieved.

6 Pour into a clean saucepan, stir in the remaining shelled mussels and reheat gently. If the soup is too thick, stir in a little milk.

7 Serve in warmed soup bowls, sprinkled with the toasted pumpkin seeds and topped with the reserved mussels in shells.

Parsley Soup

2 bunches of flat-leaf parsley
75 g (3 oz) butter
2 large leeks (white part only), sliced
1 large potato, peeled and diced
750 ml (1½ pints) chicken stock
salt and freshly ground black pepper
150 ml (¼ pint) double cream

1 Separate the parsley leaves from the stalks. Melt the butter in a saucepan, add the leeks and parsley stalks, cover and sweat gently for 20 minutes. Add the potato, chicken stock and salt and pepper. Cover and simmer for a further 20 minutes.

2 Chop half of the parsley leaves, add to the soup and simmer for a few minutes.

3 Blanch the rest of the parsley in boiling water for 10-15 seconds; drain, refresh in cold water and squeeze dry.

4 Purée the soup with the blanched parsley leaves in a blender or food processor until smooth. Pass through a fine sieve into a clean pan.

5 Add the cream and reheat gently. Check the seasoning before serving.

Cream of Garlic Soup

45 ml (3 tbsp) extra-virgin oil
1 large onion, roughly chopped
2 bulbs of garlic, separated into cloves,
   peeled and roughly chopped
2 large potatoes, peeled and diced
45 ml (3 tbsp) plain flour
1.2 litres (2 pints) hot milk
2 sage leaves
1 bay leaf
300 ml (½ pint) double cream
salt and freshly ground black pepper

To Serve:
Konafa Salad Basket (see right)

1 Heat the oil in a large, heavy-based pan, add the onion and garlic and sweat gently for about 10 minutes until soft. Add the potatoes and sprinkle over the flour. Stir and cook gently for 4-5 minutes until the flour is cooked, but not browned.

2 Gradually whisk in the hot milk, then add the sage, bay leaf and salt and pepper. Bring to the boil, lower the heat, cover and simmer for 15 minutes.

3 Discard the herbs and purée the soup in a blender or food processor, or press through a fine sieve. Return to the clean pan and add the cream. Heat slowly, stirring all the time; do not boil. Remove from the heat and check the seasoning. Serve hot accompanied by the salad basket.

Konafa Salad Basket

225 g (8 oz) konafa or filo pastry
50 g (2 oz) unsalted butter, melted
finely grated zest and juice of 1 lime
5 ml (1 tsp) honey
pinch of salt
2 plum tomatoes, diced
¼ cucumber, diced
8 black olives (optional)

1 Carefully open the konafa or filo pastry. Keep it folded and using a sharp knife, cut the pastry into very fine shreds. Pour the melted butter into a large bowl, add the konafa or filo shreds and toss until well coated.

2 Divide into 4 portions and form each into a nest-shaped basket on an oiled baking tray. Bake in a preheated oven at 230°C (450°F) mark 8 for 5 minutes until crisp and brown. Carefully transfer to a wire rack to cool.

3 In a small bowl, mix together the lime zest and juice, honey and salt to make a dressing.

4 Arrange the tomatoes, cucumber and olives if using in the baskets and place on individual serving plates. Spoon the dressing over the salad. Serve with the soup, breaking up the basket to eat with it, in place of bread.

Poached Oysters wrapped in Lettuce with a Citrus Beurre Blanc

16 oysters
16 lettuce leaves
salt and freshly ground black pepper

Stock:
700 g (1½ lb) fish bones (preferably sole)
600 ml (1 pint) water
1 bay leaf
2 shallots, chopped
60 ml (2 fl oz) dry white wine

Beurre Blanc:
90 ml (3 fl oz) white wine
juice of ½ orange
juice of ½ lemon
75-100 g (3-4 oz) unsalted butter, chilled
    and diced

1 Prepare the fish stock in advance. Put all of the ingredients in a saucepan, add seasoning and bring slowly to the boil. Skim the surface. Simmer for 20 minutes, then strain through a fine sieve and return to the cleaned pan. Boil to reduce to about 300 ml (½ pint); set aside.

2 Blanch the lettuce leaves in boiling water for 1-2 seconds only. Refresh in cold water, drain and pat dry with kitchen paper. Lay flat on a board.

3 Open the oysters and take out the meat. Scrub the bottom shells clean and place in a low oven to warm. Wrap each oyster in a lettuce leaf to make a small parcel. Bring the stock to a simmer in a wide shallow pan.

4 To make the beurre blanc, put the wine, orange juice and lemon juice into a saucepan and reduce to about 75 ml (5 tbsp). Lower the heat and gradually whisk in the butter a piece at a time, making sure each piece is incorporated before adding the next; do not allow to boil. The sauce will become thick and creamy. Season with salt and pepper to taste.

5 Add the oyster parcels to the simmering stock and poach for approximately 1 minute. Carefully drain and place each parcel in a warm oyster shell. Place on warmed serving plates and spoon the warm sauce on top of the parcels. Serve at once.

Pan-seared Scallops on Gazpacho Salsa

12 scallops, cleaned
200 ml (7 fl oz) olive oil
1 red pepper
1 yellow pepper, cored, deseeded and roughly
   chopped
2 tomatoes, skinned
handful of parsley leaves
2 cm (¾ inch) cucumber
1 clove garlic, peeled
5 ml (1 tsp) balsamic vinegar
few drops of Tabasco sauce
juice of ½ orange
juice of ½ lemon
juice of ½ lime
2.5 ml (½ tsp) tomato paste
small knob of butter
salt and freshly ground black pepper
200 g (7 oz) baby spinach
chives, to garnish

1 Put the scallops in a bowl, add half of the olive oil and set aside to marinate.

2 Grill the red pepper under a hot grill, turning occasionally, until the skin is blistered and blackened all over. Place in a covered bowl until cool enough to handle, then peel off the skin. Put the red and yellow pepper into a food processor, pulse to chop finely, then transfer to a bowl.

3 Place the skinned tomatoes, parsley, cucumber, garlic, vinegar, Tabasco and citrus juices in the food processor and pulse until finely chopped and evenly mixed. Add to the peppers and set aside to marinate for at least 30 minutes.

4 Turn the mixture into a sieve over a pan to separate the salsa from the juices. Put the salsa into a bowl and stir in the remaining 100 ml (3½ fl oz) olive oil.

5 Add the tomato paste to the juices in the pan and bring to the boil. Reduce to a sauce consistency, then whisk in the knob of butter and adjust the seasoning.

6 Meanwhile, remove any large stalks from the spinach, then place in a large colander and season with salt and pepper.

7 To cook the scallops, preheat a griddle or heavy-based frying pan. Add the scallops to the hot pan and cook for 1-2 minutes each side.

8 To cook the spinach, pour a kettleful of boiling water over the spinach, allow to drain, then dry on kitchen paper.

9 To serve, place a small mound of spinach in the middle of each warmed serving plate and top with a large spoonful of gazpacho salsa. Place 3 scallops on top of this, drizzle the sauce around and garnish with chives. Serve at once.

Crab Cakes with Pineapple and Chilli Salsa

For optimum flavour, use equal quantities of white and brown crab meat.

Crab Cakes:
400 g (14 oz) fresh crabmeat (picked over to remove any shell and cartilage)
½ red pepper, deseeded and finely chopped
1 tomato, skinned, deseeded and finely chopped
6 spring onions (white and pale green part only), finely sliced
1 celery stick, finely diced
7 g (¼ oz) parsley leaves, finely chopped
7 g (¼ oz) basil leaves, finely chopped
7.5 ml (1½ tsp) Dijon mustard
1 egg, (size 1) beaten
125 g (4 oz) soft white breadcrumbs
sea salt and freshly ground black pepper
25 g (1 oz) butter
45 ml (3 tbsp) olive oil

Salsa:
1 medium pineapple, peeled, cored and roughly chopped
½ red pepper, deseeded and finely chopped
7 g (¼ oz) mint leaves, finely chopped
1 red chilli, deseeded if preferred and finely chopped (see note)

To Garnish:
mint sprigs

1 To make the crab cakes, put the crabmeat, pepper, tomato, spring onions, celery and herbs into a large bowl and mix well. Add the mustard and beaten egg and mix again. Work in half of the breadcrumbs and season generously with salt and pepper.

2 Divide the mixture into 12 portions and shape each into a flat round patty, with your hands. Spread the rest of the breadcrumbs on a large plate. Roll each patty in the breadcrumbs until thoroughly coated, then flatten slightly. Chill in the refrigerator for at least 30 minutes before cooking.

3 For the salsa, place all the ingredients in a food processor and whizz until very finely chopped and evenly mixed; strain off excess liquid if necessary.

4 To cook the crab cakes, heat the oil and butter in a large heavy-based frying pan. When hot, fry the crab cakes for 2 minutes each side until golden brown. Drain on kitchen paper.

5 Arrange 3 crab cakes on each serving plate with a portion of salsa in the centre. Garnish with mint sprigs and serve at once.

Note: Use either a hot or mild chilli for the salsa, depending on taste. A slightly different smoky flavour can be achieved by using canned chipotle en adobo chillies.

Grilled Mussels with Pesto

60 large mussels in shells
100 ml (3½ fl oz) dry white wine
2 slices white bread, crusts removed

Pesto:
15 g (½ oz) basil leaves
2 large cloves garlic
175 ml (6 fl oz) good-quality olive oil
15 g (½ oz) Parmesan cheese, freshly grated
15 g (½ oz) pine nuts

1 Scrub the mussels thoroughly under cold running water, removing the beards. Discard any which are damaged or open and do not close when sharply tapped.

2 Place the mussels in a large pan with the wine. Cover tightly and cook over a high heat for 3-5 minutes until the shells open. Discard any mussels which have not opened. Remove the empty half shell from each mussel and discard.

3 Strain the mussel cooking liquor through a fine sieve into a small pan. Boil rapidly to reduce the liquor until only about 15 ml (1 tbsp) remains.

4 Work the bread to fine crumbs, using a blender or food processor.

5 To make the pesto, put all of the ingredients in a food processor and process briefly until roughly chopped. Add 5 ml (1 tsp) of the reduced liquor to season the pesto. Taste and add more liquor if required, a little at a time until you reach the correct flavour (bearing in mind it will be salty).

6 Lay the mussels in their half shells on the grill rack. Spoon the pesto on top, then sprinkle over the breadcrumbs. Grill under a high heat for a few minutes until the crumbs are beginning to brown. Arrange on individual plates and serve at once.

Coronet of Dover Sole filled with Shrimps, served with a Saffron Sauce

1 large Dover sole, skinned and filleted
300 ml (½ pint) fish stock
300 ml (½ pint) white wine
1 shallot, finely chopped
few drops of lime juice
few tarragon sprigs
pinch of saffron strands
60 ml (2 fl oz) double cream
salt and freshly ground pepper
25 g (1 oz) unsalted butter
125 g (4 oz) cooked shelled brown shrimps
coriander leaves, to garnish

1 Put half of the fish stock in a saucepan with the wine, shallot, lime juice and tarragon. Bring to the boil, then simmer, uncovered, for about 20 minutes until well reduced. Add a pinch of saffron and enough cream to give the desired consistency. Pass through a sieve and return to the pan. Check the seasoning.

2 Meanwhile pour the remaining stock into a wide, shallow pan and bring to a simmer. Add the 4 sole fillets and poach gently for a few minutes until opaque.

3 At the same time, heat the butter in another pan, add the shrimps and gently warm through.

4 To serve, form each sole fillet into a crown on a warmed plate and fill with the shrimps. Surround with the saffron sauce and garnish with coriander. Serve at once.

Note: Use the bones from the fish (plus a few extra sole bones if possible) to make a well-flavoured stock for the saffron sauce. For optimum flavour use freshly cooked brown shrimps.

Monkfish and Prawn Brochettes on a bed of Leeks with a Saffron Sauce

20 cooked prawns in shells
185 ml (6 fl oz) water
5 cm (2 inch) piece leek
50 ml (2 fl oz) white wine
large pinch of saffron strands
90 ml (3 fl oz) double cream
salt and freshly ground white pepper
knob of butter
225 g (8 oz) monkfish fillet, skinned
oil, for brushing

For the Leeks:
2 large leeks, trimmed
50 g (2 oz) butter

1 Set aside 4 whole prawns for garnish; shell the rest of the prawns and set aside, reserving the shells.

2 To make the saffron sauce, put the prawn shells into a saucepan with the water and piece of leek. Bring to the boil and boil steadily for about 5-10 minutes until the liquid is reduced by half.

3 Strain the stock and return to the cleaned pan. Add the wine and saffron strands and simmer until reduced by half. Add the cream and simmer gently until the sauce is thick enough to lightly coat the back of a spoon. Adjust the seasoning, then whisk in the knob of butter; keep warm.

4 To prepare the brochettes, remove all membranes from the monkfish and cut into 12 even-sized chunks. Thread onto 4 wooden brochette skewers, alternating with pairs of prawns, starting and ending with a cube of monkfish.

5 Season with salt and pepper and lightly brush with oil. Place on a grill rack and cook under a preheated grill, turning occasionally, for about 2 minutes on each side until lightly golden, turning once.

6 Meanwhile, prepare the leeks. Cut into 5 cm (2 inch) julienne. Heat the butter in a pan, add the leeks and sweat for about 5 minutes until tender.

7 Remove the leeks from the pan and pile onto the centre of each warmed serving plate. Balance a brochette on top and surround with the sauce. Garnish with the whole prawns and serve at once.

Warm Salad of Char-grilled Monkfish in a Prosciutto Parcel with a Lemon and Rosemary Dressing

1 monkfish tail
grated zest and juice of 1 lemon
30 ml (2 tbsp) light olive oil
    (approximately)
1 rosemary sprig
groundnut oil, for brushing
15 ml (1 tbsp) dark soy sauce
4 thin slices Parma ham
30 ml (2 tbsp) dry white wine
15 ml (1 tbsp) fish stock
15 ml (1 tbsp) balsamic vinegar
salt and freshly ground black pepper
1 ripe Italian tomato, skinned, deseeded and
    diced
15 ml (1 tbsp) capers

To Garnish:
selection of mixed salad leaves (eg lamb's
    lettuce, watercress)

1 Fillet the monkfish by cutting down either side of the backbone. Pull off any skin and membrane still attached. Halve each fillet and place them in a shallow dish. Add the lemon zest and juice, olive oil and rosemary. Turn the monkfish, then leave to marinate in a cool place for 2-3 hours.

2 Remove the fish from the marinade and pat dry; reserve the marinade. Preheat a ridged, cast-iron griddle or heavy-based frying pan on a medium heat. When hot, brush with a little groundnut oil and the soy sauce. Add the monkfish fillets and cook, undisturbed, for 5 minutes. Turn the fish over and cook for a further 5 minutes.

3 Remove from the pan and wrap each piece of fish in a slice of Parma ham. Return briefly to the pan and sear on all sides for about 30 seconds – to just colour the ham, not cook it. Transfer to a warmed dish, cover with foil and keep warm.

4 Turn off the heat under the pan, then strain the marinade into it. Add the white wine, fish stock and balsamic vinegar letting it sizzle and reduce slightly in the residual heat of the pan. Taste and adjust the seasoning. If the flavour is too sharp, add a little more olive oil. Add the chopped tomatoes and capers.

5 To serve, slice the monkfish fillets into medallions and arrange on warmed serving plates. Garnish with the salad leaves and pour the warm dressing over the fish.

Salad of Red Mullet and Crayfish, served with Warm Provençal Sauce and Aubergine Crisps

3 red mullet
pinch of saffron strands (optional)
4 raw crayfish
30 ml (2 tbsp) olive oil
sea salt and freshly ground black pepper

Aubergine Crisps:
1 aubergine
15 ml (1 tbsp) plain flour

Salad:
sufficient mixed salad leaves for 4 (eg frisée, lamb's lettuce, lollo rosso, rocket)

Vinaigrette:
20 ml (4 tbsp) sherry vinegar
5 ml (1 tsp) balsamic vinegar
squeeze of lemon juice
100 ml (3½ fl oz) olive oil
10 ml (2 tsp) groundnut oil

Provençal Sauce:
1 tomato, skinned, deseeded and diced
5 ml (1 tsp) diced black olives
5 ml (1 tsp) chopped basil
squeeze of lemon juice

1 Fillet each red mullet into four and rub the flesh with saffron strands if available – to impart a yellow colour.

2 Shell the crayfish and slit lengthwise along the back without cutting right through – so that they open out to form a butterfly shape. Brush with a little olive oil.

3 For the vinaigrette, in a bowl whisk the vinegars with the lemon juice and seasoning. Add the oils and whisk to a light emulsion. Check the seasoning.

4 For the Provençal sauce, mix the tomato, olives, basil and lemon juice together in a saucepan and warm gently. Season with salt and pepper to taste.

5 For the aubergine crisps, halve the aubergine lengthwise, then cut each half crosswise into thin slices. Season the flour with salt and use to dust the aubergine slices, shaking off any excess. Heat the oil for deep-frying and fry the aubergine slices for about 30 seconds until crispy and golden. Drain on kitchen paper and sprinkle with salt.

6 Heat 25 ml (5 tsp) olive oil in a large frying pan. Add the red mullet fillets, skin-side down, and fry for 2 minutes, then turn over and cook for a further 30 seconds. Remove with a fish slice, drain and keep warm. Add the crayfish to the pan and cook for 1 minute each side; drain. Meanwhile, warm the Provençal sauce.

7 To serve, toss the mixed salad leaves with the vinaigrette, then arrange a mound in the centre of each serving plate. Spoon the warm Provençal sauce in a circle around the salad leaves. Arrange three red mullet fillets and one crayfish in a ring on top of the sauce and place the aubergine crisps on top of the fish. Serve at once.

Red Mullet with Shredded Leeks and a Saffron Beurre Blanc

6 small red mullet, each about 175 g (6 oz), cleaned
4 leeks, trimmed
salt and freshly ground black pepper

Fish Stock:
reserved fish bones and tails
½ onion
handful of parsley
1 bay leaf
600 ml (1 pint) water

Saffron Beurre Blanc:
2 shallots, finely chopped
pinch of saffron strands
pinch of salt
60 ml (4 tbsp) white wine
60 ml (4 tbsp) white wine vinegar
100 g (4 oz) chilled unsalted butter, cut into 8 pieces
150 ml (¼ pint) fish stock (see above)

1 Fillet the fish, discarding the heads but reserving the bones and tails for the stock. Wrap the fillets in cling film and keep cool.

2 To make the fish stock, put the fish bones and tails, onion, parsley and bay leaf into a saucepan and pour on the water. Season lightly with salt and pepper. Bring to the boil and simmer, uncovered, for about 30 minutes. Allow to cool, then strain through a fine sieve.

3 Slice the leeks into fine rings, about 3 mm (⅛ inch) thick; set aside.

4 Start preparing the beurre blanc. Put the shallots in a pan with the saffron, salt, wine and vinegar. Bring to a fast boil, then simmer and reduce until you have a 'mush' of shallots and a thin film of residual liquid. Remove from the heat for 1 minute.

5 Season the flesh side of the fish fillets and place, skin-side up, on a lightly oiled baking sheet. Bake in a preheated oven at 200°C (400°F) mark 6 for 5 minutes or so, until the fillets are tender and cooked through.

6 Meanwhile finish the beurre blanc. Add two lumps of butter to the pan and whisk vigorously over a low heat, until combined. Add the rest of the butter, a piece at a time, making sure each piece is incorporated before adding the next. Finally stir in the fish stock, a little at a time, until the sauce is the consistency of thin cream. Check the seasoning. Keep warm over the lowest possible heat until required; do not allow to boil. Strain before serving.

7 In the meantime, steam the leeks over boiling water for 2 minutes; drain well.

8 To serve, arrange a small pile of leeks in the centre of each serving plate. Place 3 red mullet fillets on top and surround with a little of the beurre blanc. Serve at once.

Grilled Red Mullet with an Aubergine and Herb Pesto Salad

½ aubergine
olive oil, for brushing
salt and freshly ground black pepper
4 red mullet fillets, each about 75-125 g
(3-4 oz)

Pesto:
40 g (1½ oz) mixed herb leaves (basil, flat-
leaf parsley and rocket)
25 g (1 oz) Parmesan cheese, freshly grated
25 g (1 oz) pine nuts
1 clove garlic, chopped
100 ml (3½ fl oz) virgin olive oil

To Serve:
salad leaves (lollo rosso, radicchio, rocket etc)
extra-virgin olive oil
squeeze of lemon juice

1 First make the pesto. Put all of the ingredients in a blender or food processor and process for approximately 10 seconds; the mixture should be fairly coarse at this stage; remove 30 ml (2 tbsp) and set aside. Blend the remaining pesto until it is quite smooth.

2 Slice the aubergine into four 1 cm (½ inch) thick slices. Brush liberally with olive oil and season with salt. Cook under a preheated high grill until just tender, basting with more oil as necessary.

3 Brush the red mullet fillets with olive oil and season with salt and pepper. Grill for 2 minutes on each side.

4 Spread the aubergine slices with the coarse pesto and place under the grill until the pesto is warmed through.

5 Place an aubergine slice on each warmed serving plate and position a red mullet fillet alongside. Drizzle a little of the pesto over the fish and onto the plate. Serve with the salad leaves, tossed in olive oil flavoured with a little lemon juice.

Seared Medallions of Rock Salmon on a bed of Shiitake Mushrooms with Potato Wafers and a Truffle Vinaigrette

500 g (1 lb 2 oz) rock salmon, filleted
15 ml (1 tbsp) lemon juice
salt and freshly ground black pepper
120 g (4 oz) shiitake mushrooms, trimmed
15 ml (1 tbsp) light olive oil
15 ml (1 tbsp) butter

Potato Wafers:
275 ml (9 fl oz) boiling water
60 g (2 oz) instant potato flakes
1 egg white
30 ml (2 tbsp) chopped chives

Truffle Vinaigrette:
150 ml (¼ pint) light olive oil
50 ml (2 fl oz) truffle oil
50 ml (2 fl oz) whipping cream
30 ml (2 tbsp) truffle vinegar
5 ml (1 tsp) brown sugar

1 First make the potato waters. Pour the boiling water into a bowl, add the potato flakes and stir until smooth. In a separate bowl, whisk the egg white until stiff, then fold into the potato mixture. Season with salt and pepper to taste and stir in the chives. Shape the mixture into 12 small balls and place well apart on a baking tray lined with non-stick baking parchment or bake-o-glide. Dip your fingers into cold water, then flatten each ball to a thin round. Cook in the middle of a preheated oven at 180°C (350°F) mark 4 for about 6-8 minutes; check frequently to ensure the edges don't brown too quickly.

2 Meanwhile, cut the rock salmon fillets into bite-sized medallions. Drizzle with lemon juice and season with salt and pepper to taste.

3 To prepare the vinaigrette, whisk all the ingredients together in a bowl to emulsify and season with salt and pepper to taste.

4 Place the mushrooms in a heavy-based pan over a medium heat and dry-fry for a few seconds, then add the olive oil and butter. Cook until the mushrooms start to release their own moisture. Season with salt and pepper to taste.

5 Meanwhile, lay the rock salmon medallions on the grill rack and cook under a preheated medium grill for 4-5 minutes until tender, turning and basting from time to time.

6 Spoon the mushrooms onto warmed serving plates and top with the salmon medallions. Position the potato wafers on top. Whisk the truffle vinaigrette again, then drizzle around the edge of the plate.

Note: Any remaining vinaigrette can be stored in the refrigerator in a screw-topped jar for up to 1 week.

Salmon Parcels with Dill Sauce

Salmon Parcels:
60 g (2½ oz) unsalted butter
4 medium potatoes
8 dill sprigs
4 pieces skinless salmon fillets, each about
   60 g (2½ oz)
salt and freshly ground black pepper

Dill Sauce:
100 g (3½ oz) unsalted butter
60 g (2½ oz) shallots, finely chopped
30 ml (2 tbsp) chopped dill
240 ml (8 fl oz) fish stock
120 ml (4 fl oz) dry white wine
60 ml (4 tbsp) Noilly Prat (optional)
5 ml (1 tsp) lemon juice

To Garnish:
1 red pepper
10 ml (2 tsp) olive oil
dill sprigs

1 Take four microwave-proof dinner plates and stretch cling film (see note) over each one, drum-tight. Smear a little butter over each sheet of cling film.

2 Peel the potatoes and trim to give 4 cylinders, each about 5 cm (2½ inches) in diameter. Cut each one into wafer-thin slices, using a mandoline.

3 On each sheet of cling film form an overlapping circle of potato slices, 18 cm (7 inches) in diameter. Fill the centre with a potato slice. Microwave each plate in turn on HIGH for 3 minutes, then allow to cool.

4 Place a sprig of dill in the centre of each potato circle. Add a knob of butter, then cover with a salmon fillet. Top with a dill sprig and season with salt and pepper.

5 Carefully loosen the edge of the cling film and gather the four corners up over the top, drawing the potato slices up around the salmon. Twist the corners together to form tight packages. Refrigerate for at least 1 hour.

6 Meanwhile, prepare the garnish. Cut the top and bottom off the pepper, deseed, then rub the pepper skin with oil. Roast in a preheated oven at 220°C (425°F) mark 7 for about 20 minutes until blackened. Wrap in foil and leave to cool, then remove the skin and cut the pepper into fine strips.

7 To make the sauce, melt 25 g (1 oz) of the butter in a small pan, add the shallots and cook gently, without browning, for 2 minutes. Add 15 ml (1 tbsp) chopped dill and allow to wilt, then add the fish stock, white wine and Noilly Prat if using. Reduce by half, then add the rest of the dill and cook for a few seconds. Transfer to a blender or food processor and work until smooth. Pass through a sieve and return to the pan.

8 To cook the salmon parcels, remove the cling film and place the parcels in a roasting tin. Cook in a preheated oven at 220°C (425°F) mark 7 for 20 minutes.

9 To finish the sauce, reheat if necessary and whisk in the remaining butter, a small piece at a time, until a glossy sauce is obtained. Add the lemon juice and check the seasoning.

10 To serve, place a salmon parcel in the middle of each warmed serving plate. Spoon a little dill sauce around each one, then garnish with the strips of red pepper and dill. Serve immediately.

Note: Make sure you use non PVC cling film which is designated suitable for use in the microwave oven.

Seared Salmon on Wilted Baby Spinach with Lemon Grass Beurre Blanc

300 g (10 oz) salmon fillet (middle-cut), skinned
salt and freshly ground black pepper
5 ml (1 tsp) olive oil
200 g (7 oz) baby spinach leaves

Sauce:
30 ml (2 tbsp) white wine vinegar
30 ml (2 tbsp) white wine
2 shallots, finely chopped
2 lemon grass stalks, chopped
4 whole black peppercorns, crushed
200 g (7 oz) unsalted butter, chilled and cut into small cubes
juice of ½ lime, or to taste

To Garnish:
chervil sprigs
chives

1 To prepare the salmon, slice each fillet vertically into 1 cm (½ inch) thick slices. Flatten the slices lightly between two sheets of oiled cling film, using a rolling pin. Season with salt and pepper. Set aside while preparing the sauce.

2 For the sauce, put the vinegar, white wine, shallots, lemon grass and crushed peppercorns in a pan over a gentle heat and reduce by half. Gradually whisk in the chilled butter, a piece at a time, making sure each piece is incorporated before adding the next. Season with salt and pepper to taste and add the lime juice. Keep warm.

3 Immediately before serving, heat the olive oil in a pan, add the spinach leaves and cook until just wilted; keep warm. Preheat a griddle or heavy-based frying pan and sear the salmon over a high heat for about 1 minute on each side.

4 To serve, pile the spinach onto the centre of each warmed plate and arrange the slices of salmon on top. Strain the sauce and spoon around the spinach. Garnish with chervil and chives. Serve at once.

Salmon and Dill Parcels with Tomato and Fennel Salsa and a Pernod Dressing

150 g (5 oz) salmon fillet, skinned
50 g (2 oz) smoked salmon trimmings
175 g (6 oz) smoked salmon slices
1 egg (size 1)
finely grated zest of ½ lemon
salt and freshly ground black pepper
pinch of cayenne pepper
100 g (3½ oz) cream cheese
120 ml (4 fl oz) double cream
15 ml (1 tbsp) chopped dill

Salsa:
2 ripe tomatoes, skinned
½ small fennel bulb

Dressing:
45 ml (3 tbsp) olive oil
7.5 ml (1½ tsp) Pernod
15 ml (1 tbsp) lemon juice

To Garnish:
dill sprigs

1 Roughly chop the fresh salmon and smoked salmon trimmings. Place in a food processor and work until smooth. With the motor running, add the egg through the feeder tube and process until evenly blended. Transfer to a bowl and stir in the grated lemon zest. Season with salt, pepper and a pinch of cayenne. Chill in the refrigerator for 10 minutes.

2 Meanwhile, in a small bowl, mix the cream cheese with 15 ml (1 tsp) of the cream, the chopped dill and a little salt and pepper. Chill for 10 minutes.

3 Stir the rest of the cream into the salmon mixture, a spoonful at a time.

4 Line 4 ramekins with the smoked salmon slices, allowing some excess to overhang the rim. Half-fill with the salmon mixture. Place a spoonful of the cream cheese mixture in the centre of each one and top with the remaining salmon mixture. Fold the overhanging smoked salmon over the filling to enclose.

5 Stand the ramekins in a roasting tin and half-fill the tin with boiling water. Cook in a preheated oven at 170°C (325°F) mark 3 for 20 minutes until just set and firm to the touch. Remove from the tin and allow to cool to room temperature.

6 To make the salsa, halve and deseed the tomatoes, then cut the flesh into strips. Cut the fennel into thin strips and mix with the tomato.

7 Put the ingredients for the dressing in a screw-topped jar and shake vigorously to combine. Season with salt and pepper.

8 Unmould the salmon parcels onto individual serving plates and spoon the salsa alongside. Pour a little dressing over the salsa and garnish with dill to serve.

Salmon and Asparagus Pastries filled with Tomato Fondue, served with a Saffron Butter Sauce

375 g (13 oz) packet puff pastry
1 egg yolk, beaten, to glaze
salt and freshly ground black pepper
250 g (9 oz) salmon fillet (middle-cut),
  skinned and cut into 4 portions
16 baby asparagus spears

Tomato Fondue:
900 g (2 lb) tomatoes
15 g (½ oz) butter
½ onion, finely chopped
1 clove garlic, finely chopped
120 ml (4 fl oz) dry white wine
1 bouquet garni
pinch of sugar

Saffron Butter Sauce:
500 ml (16 fl oz) dry white wine
45 ml (3 tbsp) white wine vinegar
1 shallot, thinly sliced
pinch of saffron strands
175 ml (6 fl oz) double cream
60 ml (2 fl oz) crème fraîche
175 g (6 oz) unsalted butter, in pieces

1 Roll out the pastry to a 5 mm (¼ inch) thickness, brush with beaten egg yolk to glaze and set aside.

2 To make the tomato fondue, immerse the tomatoes in a bowl of boiling water for about 30 seconds, then drain and peel away the skins. Halve and deseed the tomatoes, then chop the flesh finely. Melt the butter in a heavy-based frying pan, add the onion and garlic and sauté until softened. Add the diced tomatoes, wine, bouquet garni and sugar. Cook, uncovered, for 15-20 minutes, stirring occasionally until the mixture resembles a thick paste. Season with salt and pepper to taste. Set aside.

3 Using a 7.5 cm (3 inch) cutter, cut out 4 rounds from the pastry and decorate each one by etching a leaf pattern with a skewer or the point of a knife. Bake in a preheated oven at 220°C (425°F) mark 7 for 10-15 minutes until well risen and golden brown.

4 Meanwhile, make the sauce. Put the wine, vinegar, shallot and saffron in a pan and bring to the boil. Let bubble until reduced by half. Add the cream and crème fraîche and reduce by one third. Pass the sauce through a fine sieve into a heatproof bowl and set over a pan of simmering water. Whisk in the butter, a piece at a time, making sure each piece is incorporated before adding the next. Once all the butter is incorporated the sauce should have thickened slightly. Keep warm; do not allow to boil.

5 Season the salmon fillets with salt and pepper and cook under a preheated hot grill for 2-3 minutes each side until tender.

6 Meanwhile cook the asparagus in boiling water for a few minutes until just tender; drain. Reheat the pastries in a warm oven; reheat the tomato fondue.

7 To assemble, split each pastry in half and fill with the tomato mixture. Place on warmed serving plates, positioning the pastries slightly off centre. Cut each salmon portion into 3 strips and arrange alternately on each plate with the asparagus spears. Pour over the sauce and serve immediately.

Confit of Salmon on Potato Pancake with Anchovy Cream

4 salmon fillets, each about 125 g (4 oz),
  skinned
50 g (2 oz) smoked salmon slices
  (approximately)
350 g (12 oz) duck fat (approximately)
salt and freshly ground black pepper

Potato Pancakes:
250 g (9 oz) floury potato
30 ml (2 tbsp) plain flour
1 egg (size 1)
30 ml (2 tbsp) double cream
  (approximately)
25 g (1 oz) butter

Anchovy Cream:
2 cloves garlic, crushed
2 egg yolks
5 ml (1 tsp) Dijon mustard
10 ml (2 tsp) white wine vinegar
120-150 ml (4-5 fl oz) olive oil
4 anchovy fillets, puréed

To Garnish:
¼ cucumber, skinned, deseeded and cut into
  julienne
a little white wine vinegar

1 Trim the slices of smoked salmon to the same dimensions as the fresh salmon fillets; set aside.

2 To prepare the garnish, sprinkle the cucumber with salt and leave to stand for 20 minutes. Rinse, drain and pat dry with kitchen paper, then toss in a little wine vinegar.

3 To make the pancake batter, peel and dice the potato, then cook in boiling salted water until tender. Drain and mash until smooth; let cool. Stir in the flour, then the egg and beat until smooth. Add enough cream to give a batter consistency. Check the seasoning.

4 To make the anchovy cream, whisk the garlic, egg yolks, mustard and vinegar together in a bowl. Slowly add the olive oil, whisking constantly until a thick mayonnaise is obtained. Stir in the puréed anchovy.

5 Heat the duck fat in a shallow pan, add the salmon fillets and poach for 5-10 minutes until just cooked. Drain off the fat.

6 Meanwhile, heat a blini pan or small crêpe pan and add a knob of the butter. When sizzling, pour in sufficient batter to cover the base of the pan. Cook for about 2 minutes, then place in a preheated oven at 180°C (350°F) mark 4 for 3-4 minutes to 'set' the pancake. Flip the pancake over and return to the hob. Cook for 1-2 minutes until the underside is golden brown. Repeat with the remaining batter to make 4 pancakes in total; keep warm.

7 To serve, place a potato pancake in the centre of each serving plate. Lay a salmon steak on top and cover with a slice of smoked salmon. Drizzle the anchovy cream around the plate, garnish with strips of marinated cucumber and serve at once.

Grilled Chicken Liver Salad

For this starter, you will need 8 small wooden skewers. Pre-soak them in cold water for 30 minutes to prevent scorching during cooking.

225 g (8 oz) chicken livers
juice of 1 lemon
30 ml (2 tbsp) soy sauce
225 g (8 oz) watercress, stalks removed
2 large oranges
5 ml (1 tsp) oil

1 Wash the chicken livers and pat dry with kitchen paper. Cut into small chunks, discarding any discoloured or stringy bits. Place the livers in a small bowl, add the lemon juice and soy sauce and stir well. Cover and leave to marinate in the refrigerator for at least 30 minutes.

2 Roughly chop the watercress leaves, and arrange on 4 serving plates.

3 Peel the oranges, removing all the pith, then carefully cut the segments free from the membrane. Set aside 8 segments for garnish; roughly chop the remainder and scatter over the watercress.

4 Preheat a griddle pan and lightly brush with the oil. (Alternatively, preheat the grill, brushing the grill rack with oil.)

5 Remove the livers from the marinade and thread onto 8 small wooden kebab skewers. Griddle (or grill) for 5 minutes, turning two or three times, until browned on all sides but still pink in the centre.

6 Bring the marinade to the boil in a small pan and spoon over the watercress to wilt it. Place 2 skewers on top of each portion and serve immediately, garnished with the reserved orange segments.

Smoked Breast of Pigeon with Hazelnut-scented Tagliatelle and Honey and Coriander Sauce

For this starter you will need to prepare the hydromel (see right) at least 2 weeks in advance. You also require a smoker to cook the pigeon.

2 wood pigeons

Pasta:
125 g (4 oz) plain flour
1 medium egg, plus 1 egg yolk
10 ml (2 tsp) hazelnut oil
salt and freshly ground black pepper

Sauce:
125 g (4 oz) onion
125 g (4 oz) celeriac
125 g (4 oz) carrot
50 g (2 oz) mushrooms
15 ml (1 tbsp) oil
2 pigeon carcasses, chopped
2 large thyme sprigs
30 ml (2 tbsp) red wine vinegar
120 ml (4 fl oz) hydromel (see right)
300 ml (½ pint) chicken stock
30 ml (2 tbsp) rich soy sauce
25 g (1 oz) unsalted butter, chilled and diced
16 coriander leaves

Smoking:
45 ml (3 tbsp) oak chippings
10 ml (2 tsp) coriander seeds
30 ml (2 tbsp) hydromel (see right)

1 Carefully remove the breasts from the wood pigeons and set aside. (Chop the carcasses and reserve for the sauce.)

2 To make the pasta dough, place all the ingredients in a food processor and process until a smooth dough is formed. Wrap in cling film and leave to rest in the refrigerator for at least 30 minutes.

3 Meanwhile for the sauce, roughly chop the vegetables. Put the oil in a roasting tin and spread to give a thin film. Add the vegetables, pigeon carcasses and thyme. Roast in a preheated oven at 240°C (475°F) mark 9 for about 20 minutes until nicely browned.

4 Deglaze the roasting tin with the red wine vinegar and hydromel and reduce until syrupy. Add the chicken stock and soy sauce and simmer for 40 minutes.

5 Using a pasta machine, roll out the pasta dough thinly, then cut into tagliatelle. Hang over a wooden pole or pasta drier to dry until ready to cook.

6 Strain the sauce through a muslin-lined sieve into a clean pan. Reheat and whisk in the butter, a piece at a time. Season with salt and pepper to taste; keep warm.

7 To smoke the pigeon breasts, place the oak chippings and coriander seeds in the base of the smoker and put 30 ml (2 tbsp) hydromel in the liquid tray. Skin the pigeon breasts, put them in the smoking basket and smoke for 5 minutes.

8 Meanwhile, add the tagliatelle to a large pan of boiling salted water and cook for about 2 minutes until *al dente*; drain thoroughly.

9 To serve, place a small pile of tagliatelle in the centre of each warmed serving plate. Carve each pigeon breast into 5 slices and arrange on top of the pasta. Spoon the sauce around and float the coriander leaves on the sauce. Serve immediately.

Hydromel: Dry-fry 30 ml (2 tbsp) coriander seeds in a heavy-based pan for 2 minutes until they begin to release their aroma. Transfer to a large bowl and add 250 g (9 oz) thin honey; a large strip of pared orange zest; 250 ml (8 fl oz) brandy and 2 litres (3½ pints) Sauternes. Stir well, then pot in sterilised jars. Cover tightly and allow to steep for 2 weeks. Strain through muslin into sterilised bottles and cork. Store in a cool place until needed.

Smoked Chicken with Toasted Almonds, Avocado and Tomato Concassé and a Mixed Leaf Salad

175-225 g (6-8 oz) smoked skinless chicken breast
1 ripe avocado, diced
juice of ½ lemon
2 large ripe tomatoes, peeled, deseeded and diced
salt and freshly ground black pepper
pinch of sugar
a little shredded basil
1 bag mixed salad leaves (containing radicchio, rocket and other interesting leaves)
50 g (2 oz) flaked almonds, toasted

Vinaigrette:
pinch of salt
30 ml (2 tbsp) plum vinegar
5 ml (1 tsp) Dijon mustard
5 ml (1 tsp) preserved stem ginger in syrup, cut into thin shreds
5 ml (1 tsp) ginger syrup (from the jar)
freshly ground black pepper
120 ml (8 tbsp) olive oil

1 Cut the smoked chicken into julienne strips.

2 Peel, halve and stone the avocado, then dice the flesh and toss in the lemon juice to prevent discolouration.

3 Season the diced tomatoes with salt, pepper and a pinch of sugar; flavour with a little basil.

4 To make the vinaigrette, dissolve the salt in the plum vinegar, then add the mustard, ginger and syrup, pepper and oil. Whisk to emulsify.

5 Arrange the salad leaves on individual serving plates. Top with the chicken, drained avocado and tomato concassé. Drizzle with the vinaigrette and scatter over the toasted flaked almonds. Serve immediately, with warm country bread.

Note: Plum vinegar is available from some delicatessens. If unobtainable, use balsamic vinegar instead.

Wild Mushroom Risotto with Rocket

350 g (12 oz) mixed wild mushrooms
 (chanterelle, shiitake, pied à mouton etc)
60 ml (4 tbsp) olive oil
50 g (2 oz) butter
1 clove garlic, chopped or crushed
2 shallots, finely chopped
225 g (8 oz) Carnaroli or other risotto rice
2 glasses dry white vermouth or white wine
600 ml (1 pint) vegetable or chicken stock
90 ml (3 fl oz) double cream
50 g (2 oz) Parmesan or pecorino cheese,
 freshly grated
2 handfuls of rocket leaves, any thick stalks
 removed
salt and freshly ground black pepper

1 Halve or thickly slice the mushrooms if large, otherwise leave whole. Heat half of the oil and butter in a frying pan with the garlic. Add the mushrooms and fry quickly for 1-2 minutes; they should remain firm in texture. Remove from the heat; set aside.

2 Heat the remaining oil and butter in another pan. Add the shallots and fry until translucent but not brown. Add the rice and stir to ensure each grain is coated with oil and butter. Increase the heat, add the vermouth or wine and stir until it is almost completely evaporated. Meanwhile heat the stock in another saucepan and keep at a low simmer.

3 Add a ladleful of the hot stock to the rice and leave to simmer for about 5 minutes. Continue to add the stock, a ladleful at a time until the rice is cooked, allowing each addition to be absorbed before adding the next; stir frequently to make sure the rice does not stick to the pan. This should take 18-20 minutes; the rice is ready when it is *al dente*, tender but still with a 'bite' to it; do not overcook.

4 Return the mushrooms to the pan. Quickly stir in the cream, grated cheese and rocket leaves, moistening with a little more wine or vermouth if necessary. Season with salt and plenty of pepper to taste. Serve immediately.

Asparagus Risotto on a bed of Artichoke Hearts, with an Artichoke and Tomato Salsa

125 g (4 oz) green asparagus
4 large artichoke hearts (fresh or canned)
1 bouillon cube
900 ml (1½ pints) boiling water
25 g (1 oz) butter
1 small onion, thinly sliced
75 g (3 oz) Arborio rice
1 glass white wine (optional)
25-50 g (1-2 oz) Parmesan cheese, freshly grated
salt and freshly ground black pepper

Artichoke and Tomato Salsa:
4 canned artichoke hearts
2 ripe plum tomatoes, skinned
3 spring onions, trimmed
7.5 ml (½ tbsp) balsamic vinegar
15 ml (1 tbsp) olive oil
15 ml (1 tbsp) walnut oil
5 ml (1 tsp) wholegrain mustard

1 First make the salsa. Chop the artichokes, tomatoes and spring onions very finely and gently mix together in a bowl. Season generously with salt and pepper. Put the vinegar, oils and mustard in a screw-topped jar and shake vigorously to emulsify. Add the dressing to the salsa and toss lightly to mix.

2 Trim any white part from the base of the asparagus spears and peel the tough skin from the lower end of the stalks; reserve the trimmings and peelings. Cut about 5 cm (2 inches) off the tips for the garnish.

3 If using fresh artichokes, prepare them at this stage: Break off the stalks and trim away all large leaves to expose the soft heart; discard the hairy chokes.

4 To prepare the stock, dissolve the bouillon cube in the boiling water in a saucepan. Add the asparagus peelings and trimmings to impart extra flavour. Blanch the asparagus stalks in the simmering stock for 2 minutes; remove with a slotted spoon and chop finely. Add the asparagus tips to the stock and cook until just tender; drain and set aside. Strain the stock and return to the pan; keep at a low simmer.

5 Melt half of the butter in a medium saucepan, add the onion and sweat gently until softened and translucent. Add the blanched asparagus stalks and toss for a minute or two. Add the rice and stir to coat with the butter. Then gradually add the simmering stock, a ladleful at a time, allowing each addition to be absorbed before adding the next. Continue adding stock in this way, and the wine if using, until the rice is *al dente* – tender but firm to the bite and the risotto has a creamy consistency. This will take about 20-25 minutes.

6 In the meantime, cook fresh artichoke hearts in a little of the remaining stock for 5-10 minutes until tender; drain.

7 Remove the risotto from the heat, add the grated Parmesan and remaining butter. Season with salt and pepper to taste.

8 To serve, briefly warm the artichoke hearts and asparagus tips in the remaining stock; drain. Place the artichoke hearts on warmed serving plates and pile the risotto on top. Garnish with the asparagus tips and serve at once, with the salsa.

Mushroom Risotto with a Herb Salad and Parmesan Cracknel

50 g (2 oz) Parmesan cheese, freshly grated
25 g (1 oz) dried ceps
75-100 g (3-4 oz) butter, to taste
4 shallots, finely diced
225 g (8 oz) Arborio rice
1.2 litres (2 pints) hot vegetable stock
salt and freshly ground black pepper
30 ml (2 tbsp) chopped basil
45 ml (3 tbsp) chopped tarragon
45 ml (3 tbsp) chopped flat-leaf parsley
10 ml (2 tsp) extra-virgin olive oil
5 ml (1 tsp) white wine vinegar

1 First make the Parmesan cracknel. Sprinkle the cheese onto a greased baking sheet to form 4 rounds, using a 7.5 cm (3 inch) pastry cutter as a guide. Place in a preheated oven at 180°C (350°F) mark 4 for about 5 minutes until melted. Let cool slightly, then carefully transfer to a wire rack to cool completely.

2 Soak the dried ceps in warm water to cover for 20 minutes, then drain and chop, reserving the liquid.

3 Melt 25 g (1 oz) of the butter in a medium saucepan, add the shallots and sweat gently until softened. Add the ceps and sauté for 1-2 minutes.

4 Add the rice and stir until coated in the butter. Stir in the reserved mushroom liquid. Then gradually add the stock, a ladleful at a time, allowing each addition to be absorbed before adding the next, until the rice is tender and a creamy consistency is achieved. Add the remaining butter and season with salt and pepper to taste.

5 To serve, divide the risotto between 4 large soup bowls. Mix the herbs together and toss in the oil and vinegar, shape roughly into 4 balls and place on top of the risotto. Balance a Parmesan cracknel on top of the herbs and serve at once.

Wild Mushroom and Swede Ravioli with a Green Walnut Dressing

25 g (1 oz) butter
1 shallot, diced
150 g (5 oz) mixed mushrooms (chanterelles, shiitake, brown-cap etc), finely chopped
5 ml (1 tsp) chopped tarragon
5 ml (1 tsp) chopped parsley
salt and freshly ground black pepper
1 small swede, peeled
2.5 ml (½ tsp) tarragon vinegar

Dressing:
175 ml (6 fl oz) extra-virgin olive oil
15 ml (1 tbsp) chopped parsley
pinch of crushed dried chilli flakes
25 g (1 oz) chopped walnuts
1 tomato, skinned, seeded and diced
1 clove garlic, crushed

To Garnish:
tarragon sprigs

1 Melt the butter in a pan, add the shallot and mushrooms and fry gently for 1 minute. Take off the heat and add the tarragon, parsley and seasoning to taste.

2 Using a mandoline or food processor fitted with a fine slicing disc, cut 24 paper-thin slices from the swede. Using a 6 cm (2 ½ inch) cutter, stamp out 24 rounds from the slices.

3 Blanch these swede slices in boiling salted water with the tarragon vinegar added for 30 seconds only. Drain and refresh in cold water, then drain and pat dry with kitchen paper.

4 Lay half of the swede slices on a clean surface. Spoon a small mound of mushroom mixture onto the centre of each one. Position the other swede slices on top and press the edges together to seal.

5 Place the ravioli parcels in a steamer over boiling water and cook for 6-8 minutes until tender.

6 Meanwhile put all the ingredients for the dressing into a screw-topped jar and shake well to combine.

7 To serve, drain the ravioli and arrange three overlapping in the middle of each warmed plate. Spoon over the dressing. Garnish with tarragon and serve at once.

Note: Use a mixture of whichever wild mushrooms are in season.

Wild Mushrooms on Parmesan Sablés with Dressed Bitter Leaves

Pastry:
75 g (3 oz) plain flour
75 g (3 oz) butter, softened
75 g (3 oz) Parmesan cheese, freshly grated
7.5 ml (1½ tbsp) Dijon mustard

For the Mushrooms:
200 g (7 oz) mixed mushrooms (see note)
15 ml (1 tbsp) olive oil
1 clove garlic, finely chopped
15 ml (1 tbsp) mushroom ketchup
salt and freshly ground black pepper
Parmesan cheese shavings
few chives

Salad:
½ bag of mixed salad leaves (radicchio, baby spinach, rocket etc)
15 ml (1 tbsp) olive oil
30 ml (2 tbsp) balsamic vinegar
2 tomatoes, skinned, deseeded and finely chopped

1 To make the sablé pastry, sift the flour into a bowl and rub in the butter using your fingertips. Stir in the cheese and mustard and press together to form a soft dough. Wrap in cling film and chill in the refrigerator for 30 minutes.

2 Roll out the sablé pastry thinly on a lightly floured surface and use to line four 7.5 cm (3 inch) tartlet tins. Line with greaseproof paper and baking beans and bake in a preheated oven at 190°C (375°F) mark 5 for 10 minutes. Remove the paper and beans and bake for a further 5 minutes or until the pastry is crisp and golden.

3 For the mushrooms, heat the olive oil in a frying pan, add the garlic and fry gently until soft. Add the mushrooms and toss until tender but not browned. Stir in the mushroom ketchup, salt and pepper. Pile into the sablé cases and top with Parmesan shavings and chives.

4 Arrange the salad leaves in a circle on each serving plate and place a tartlet in the centre. In a bowl, mix together the olive oil, balsamic vinegar and chopped tomatoes to make a dressing; season with salt and pepper to taste. Spoon the dressing over the salad leaves and serve.

Note: If possible, use chanterelles, pied de mouton or other wild mushrooms in season. If unobtainable, use a mixture of cultivated mushrooms, such as chestnut mushrooms, shiitake etc.

Twice-baked Goat's Cheese Soufflé with a Wild Mushroom Cream Sauce

Soufflé:

150 ml (¼ pint) milk
15 g (½ oz) cornflour
3 egg yolks (size 3)
30 g (1 oz) goat's cheese
salt and freshly ground black pepper
1.25 ml (¼ tsp) paprika
1.25 ml (¼ tsp) dry mustard
4 egg whites (size 3)
juice of ½ lemon
pinch of sugar
15 g (½ oz) toasted breadcrumbs, or freshly
    grated Parmesan cheese

Sauce:

25 g (1 oz) clarified butter
60 g (2 oz) shallots, finely chopped
120 g (4 oz) mixed wild mushrooms,
    chopped
200 ml (7 fl oz) double cream
75 ml (5 tbsp) sherry vinegar
50 ml (2 fl oz) truffle oil

To Serve:

sufficient mixed salad leaves for 4 (eg rocket,
    lamb's lettuce, radicchio)
few chives, to garnish

1 Bring the milk to the boil in a saucepan. Meanwhile, beat the cornflour and egg yolks together in a bowl. Pour on a little of the hot milk, stirring all the time, then stir this mixture into the hot milk in the pan. Bring back to a simmer and cook for 2 minutes, stirring constantly.

2 Add the goat's cheese, salt, pepper, paprika and mustard and stir until smooth. Allow to cool, then weigh 265 g (9 oz) mixture and use this for the soufflé.

3 In another bowl, whisk the egg whites with the lemon juice and pinch of sugar until they form soft peaks. Stir a spoonful of the whisked egg whites into the cooled goat's cheese mixture to lighten it, then carefully fold in the rest.

4 Butter 4 ramekins and coat with toasted breadcrumbs or Parmesan cheese.

5 Divide the soufflé mixture between the ramekins. Stand in a bain-marie (or roasting tin containing enough hot water to come halfway up the sides of the dishes). Bake in a preheated oven at 160°C (325°F) mark 3 for 20-25 minutes until crisp on top.

6 Remove from the bain-marie and let cool for 4-5 minutes, then carefully ease each soufflé away from the edge of the ramekin and turn out onto a baking tray; set aside until ready to serve.

7 To make the sauce, heat the clarified butter in a pan, add the shallots and sauté until softened. Add the wild mushrooms and sauté for a few minutes. Allow to cool.

8 Lightly whip the cream in a bowl until it is a thick pouring consistency. Add the sherry vinegar, truffle oil and cooled mushroom mixture.

9 When ready to serve, arrange the salad leaves in the middle of 4 serving plates. Bake the soufflés in a preheated oven at 220°C (425°F) mark 7 for 8-10 minutes. Meanwhile, gently reheat the sauce. Place a soufflé on each bed of salad leaves, surround with the sauce and garnish with chives. Serve immediately.

Grilled Vegetables with Polenta and Pesto Dressing

3 small aubergines
1 large red pepper
1 large yellow pepper
2 courgettes
2 red onions
60 ml (4 tbsp) olive oil
15 ml (1 tbsp) balsamic vinegar
salt and freshly ground black pepper

Polenta:
375 ml (13 fl oz) vegetable stock
125 g (4 oz) polenta
25 g (1 oz) butter
50 g (2 oz) Parmesan or pecorino cheese,
    freshly grated

Pesto Dressing:
25 g (1 oz) basil leaves
1 large clove garlic, peeled
15 ml (1 tbsp) pine nuts
25 g (1 oz) pecorino or Parmesan cheese,
    freshly grated
120 ml (4 fl oz) olive oil

To Garnish:
Parmesan cheese shavings
basil sprigs

1 First make the polenta. Bring the stock to the boil in a medium heavy-based saucepan over a high heat. Add the polenta in a thin stream, whisking all the time. Lower the heat and leave to simmer for 40 minutes - 1 hour, stirring frequently. When cooked, beat in the butter, grated cheese and seasoning to taste. Turn onto a board and spread to a rectangle about 1 cm (½ inch) thick. Leave to cool.

2 To make the pesto dressing, pound the basil, garlic and pine nuts together to a paste, using a pestle and mortar or a food processor. Add the cheese and mix thoroughly. Slowly add the olive oil, stirring continuously. Season with salt to taste.

3 Cut the aubergines lengthwise into 5 mm (¼ inch) slices, sprinkle with salt, layer in a colander and leave to degorge for about 30 minutes. Quarter the peppers lengthwise and remove the cores and seeds. Slice the courgettes lengthwise into 5 mm (¼ inch) thick slices. Slice the onions into 5 mm (¼ inch) thick rounds.

4 Rinse the aubergines and pat dry with kitchen paper. Brush all the vegetables with olive oil and cook in turn under a preheated hot grill until beginning to soften, turning occasionally and basting with the oil.

5 Transfer the grilled vegetables to a platter and sprinkle with the balsamic vinegar and seasoning. Leave to marinate for 20-30 minutes.

6 Just before serving, warm the vegetables through in a moderate oven for 5-10 minutes. Preheat a griddle or lightly oiled heavy-based frying pan. Cut the polenta into triangles or diamonds, add to the griddle or pan and cook over a high heat for about 1 minute each side until lightly browned.

7 Arrange the 'toasted' polenta on warmed serving plates and arrange the warm vegetables on top. Garnish with Parmesan shavings and basil sprigs. Drizzle the pesto dressing around the edge of the plates and serve at once.

Caramelised Onion and Roasted Red Pepper Stack with Tomato and Basil Salsa

5-6 basil leaves, finely chopped
50 g (2 oz) unsalted butter, melted
4 sheets of filo pastry
1 large red pepper, quartered, cored and
    deseeded
30 ml (2 tbsp) olive oil
salt and freshly ground black pepper
225 g (8 oz) shallots, quartered
30 ml (2 tbsp) wild flower honey
30 ml (2 tbsp) balsamic vinegar
5 ml (1 tbsp) white wine vinegar

Tomato and Basil Salsa:
4 large plum tomatoes, skinned, deseeded
    and diced
½ red chilli, deseeded and finely chopped
1 clove garlic, crushed
juice of 2 limes
30 ml (2 tbsp) olive oil
12-15 basil leaves, finely chopped

To Garnish:
basil sprigs

1 Add the chopped basil leaves to the melted butter. Brush the sheets of filo pastry with this mixture and layer on top of one another. Cut out twelve 6 cm (2½ inch) circles through the quadruple thickness.

2 Transfer to a baking sheet and bake in a preheated oven at 190°C (375°F) mark 5 for 10-15 minutes until golden brown. Carefully transfer to a wire rack and leave to cool.

3 Brush the red pepper with olive oil and roast in the oven for 20 minutes until soft. Press through a nylon sieve into a bowl, season with salt and pepper to taste and leave to cool.

4 Separate the quartered shallots into their layers and place in a small baking tin. Mix together the honey and vinegars and drizzle over the shallots. Bake in the oven for 20-25 minutes until softened and golden brown.

5 Meanwhile, in a small bowl mix together the ingredients for the salsa and season with salt and pepper to taste. Cover and chill in the refrigerator until needed.

6 To serve, spread a little red pepper purée on 4 pastry rounds, then top with a layer of caramelised shallots. Repeat these layers twice, then top with the remaining pastry rounds. Serve garnished with basil and accompanied by the tomato and basil salsa.

Boursin, Roquefort and Walnut Tarts on a Salad of Baby Leaves with a Bacon and Walnut Dressing

10 sheets of filo pastry (approximately)
50 g (2 oz) butter, melted

Filling:
120 ml (4 oz) Boursin cheese
120 ml (4 oz) Roquefort cheese, crumbled
30 ml (2 tbsp) chopped walnuts
1 small leek, chopped
1 egg
120 ml (4 fl oz) double cream
salt and freshly ground black pepper
paprika, to taste

Salad:
4 rashers streaky bacon, derinded
30 ml (2 tbsp) olive oil
30 ml (2 tbsp) walnut oil
15 ml (1 tbsp) sherry vinegar
2.5 ml (½ tsp) wholegrain mustard, to taste
30 ml (2 tbsp) chopped walnuts
selection of leaves for 4 (eg baby spinach, lamb's lettuce, watercress, rocket)

1 Butter four 7.5 cm (3 inch) individual flan tins. Cut the filo pastry into twenty 11 cm (4½ inch) squares. Layer 5 squares of filo in each tin, arranging them at an angle to each other and brushing each layer generously with melted butter. The overhanging points of the filo will form a star shape.

2 Carefully invert each flan over the base of an upturned ramekin. Bake in a preheated oven at 200°C (400°F) mark 6 for 5 minutes. Remove from the ramekins and place the right way up on a wire rack to cool.

3 For the filling, in a bowl cream the Boursin and Roquefort together, then mix with the walnuts. Heat the remaining butter in a pan and gently fry the chopped leek for 2-3 minutes; let cool slightly.

4 Whisk the egg and cream together with pepper and paprika to taste; add a little salt if required (bearing in mind the cheeses are quite salty). Add to the cheese mixture with the sautéed leek and stir well.

5 Spoon the filling into the filo baskets and bake in the oven for approximately 15 minutes, taking care to ensure the pastry doesn't brown too quickly; if necessary protect the pastry rim with foil.

6 Meanwhile prepare the salad. Grill the bacon until very crisp, then cut into small pieces. For the dressing, shake the oils, vinegar and mustard together in a screw-topped jar until well mixed, then add the walnuts.

7 To serve, place a tartlet in the centre of each serving plate and surround with the salad leaves. Drizzle the dressing over the leaves, then sprinkle with the crispy bacon. Serve at once.

Carrot and Coriander Tart

Pastry:
100 g (4 oz) plain flour
pinch of salt
25 g (1 oz) butter, in pieces
25 g (1 oz) beef dripping, in pieces
1 egg yolk
5-10 ml (1-2 tsp) water

Filling:
175 g (6 oz) peeled carrots
salt and freshly ground black pepper
60 ml (2 fl oz) milk (approximately)
15 ml (1 tbsp) melted butter
1 egg, separated
5 ml (1 tsp) orange flower water
5 ml (1 tsp) ground coriander

1 To make the pastry, put the flour, salt, butter and dripping into a food processor and process until the mixture resembles fine breadcrumbs. Add the egg yolk and sufficient water to give a soft dough, adding the water gradually and processing briefly until the dough comes away from the side of the bowl. Turn the dough onto a lightly floured surface and knead lightly until smooth. Gather into a ball, wrap in cling film and leave to rest in the refrigerator for 1 hour.

2 To make the filling, cut the carrots into even-sized pieces and cook in as little boiling salted water as possible until tender; do not overcook. Drain, reserving the cooking liquid; make this up to 150 ml (¼ pint) with milk. Place the carrots in a food processor with the melted butter, egg yolk, orange flower water, coriander and milk mixture. Work to a purée and check the seasoning.

3 Divide the pastry into 4 equal pieces and roll each out to a 15 cm (6 inch) round. Line four greased 11 cm (4½ inch) loose-bottomed flan tins with the pastry, trimming the edges. Prick the bases.

4 Line with greaseproof paper and baking beans and bake blind in a preheated oven at 200°C (400°F) mark 6 for 15 minutes. Remove the paper and beans and return to the oven for a further 5 minutes until golden and crisp.

5 Whisk the egg white until stiff and fold into the carrot mixture. Divide the filling between the pastry cases and bake for a further 20 minutes or until the filling is risen and set. Serve immediately.

Note: If preferred, omit the dripping from the pastry and increase the quantity of butter to 50 g (2 oz).

Grilled Goat's Cheese Salad with Roasted Plum Tomatoes and Basil Dressing

10 small ripe plum tomatoes, skinned and
  halved
60 ml (4 tbsp) olive oil
salt and freshly ground black pepper
sufficient salad leaves for 4 (eg lamb's lettuce,
  rocket, lollo rosso)
5 ml (1 tsp) balsamic vinegar
30 ml (2 tbsp) shredded basil leaves
4 small firm goat's cheeses (eg Crottin de
  Chavignol)

1 Place the tomatoes on a shallow baking tray and drizzle with 15 ml (1 tbsp) of the olive oil. Season generously with salt and pepper. Roast in a preheated oven at 190°C (375°F) mark 5 for 1 hour.

2 Arrange the salad leaves on individual serving plates. To make the dressing, whisk the remaining olive oil with the balsamic vinegar, basil and salt and pepper to taste.

3 Approximately 5 minutes before the tomatoes finish cooking, preheat the grill and line the grill pan with lightly oiled foil. Halve each cheese horizontally to give two discs and grill until just starting to melt.

4 Arrange the roasted tomatoes on the salad leaves and place the cheese in the middle. Add any juices from the tomatoes to the dressing, then drizzle over the salad. Serve at once.

Warm Salad of Wild Mushrooms and Shallots with a Sesame Dressing

16 shallots, halved
45 ml (3 tbsp) olive oil
2 cloves garlic, peeled
sea salt flakes and freshly ground black
    pepper
175-225 g (6-8 oz) chanterelle mushrooms,
    trimmed
15 g (½ oz) butter
150 g (5 oz) mixed baby salad leaves
    (including rocket, lamb's lettuce and
    spinach)

Dressing:
15 ml (1 tbsp) toasted sesame seeds
7.5 ml (1½ tsp) sesame oil
7.5 ml (1½ tsp) white wine vinegar

To Garnish:
25 g (1 oz) Parmesan cheese, freshly pared
    into long, thin shavings

1 Put the shallots in a roasting tin with 30 ml (2 tbsp) olive oil and the whole garlic cloves. Season with salt and pepper. Roast in a preheated oven at 190°C (375°F) mark 5, turning occasionally, for 15-20 minutes, until the shallots are golden brown, tender and sweet.

2 Heat the remaining olive oil in a frying pan. Add the mushrooms and fry lightly for 3-4 minutes, then add the butter and cook for a further 2 minutes. Remove from the heat and keep warm, reserving the pan juices.

3 To prepare the dressing, toast the sesame seeds in a dry frying pan over a moderate heat until lightly browned. In a bowl, whisk together the sesame oil, toasted seeds, wine vinegar and reserved pan juices (from the mushrooms). Season with salt and pepper to taste.

4 Toss the salad leaves in the dressing, then divide between individual serving plates. Pile the mushrooms and shallots on top, distributing them evenly. Top with the slivers of Parmesan and serve at once.

Salad of Sweet Pickled Apple, Watercress and Deep-fried Goat's Cheese in a Couscous and Walnut Crust

75 g (3 oz) packet watercress
120 ml (4 fl oz) grapeseed oil
50 g (2 oz) couscous
salt and freshly ground black pepper
40 g (1½ oz) walnuts, coarsely crushed
two 100 g (3½ oz) goat's cheeses (eg crottin de chavignol)
plain flour, for dusting
1 egg, (size 3), beaten
3 Granny Smith apples
25 g (1 oz) unsalted butter
25 g (1 oz) caster sugar
30 ml (2 tbsp) cider vinegar
120 ml (4 fl oz) dry cider
grapeseed oil, for shallow-frying
5 ml (1 tsp) balsamic vinegar

1 Put half of the watercress in a blender or food processor with the grapeseed oil and process until smooth. Pour into a bowl, cover and leave to infuse for several hours, or overnight if possible.

2 Put the couscous in a shallow bowl, add just sufficient boiling water to cover and leave to soak for a few minutes until the liquid is absorbed. Fluff up the couscous with a fork, then spread the grains out on a baking sheet and leave to dry in a warm place for about 20 minutes; they shouldn't be completely dried out. Season with salt and pepper to taste, then mix with the crushed walnuts.

3 Halve each goat's cheese horizontally to make 4 rounds. Roll each one in the flour to coat evenly, then dip into the beaten egg and finally roll in the couscous mixture, making sure that all sides are well covered. Wrap each cheese tightly in cling film and refrigerate for at least 1 hour before cooking; this helps to bind the crust to the cheese. Remove the cling film just before frying.

4 Peel, core and thickly slice the apples. Melt the butter in a large non-stick frying pan over a gentle heat. Add the apples and turn to coat with the butter. Increase the heat, sprinkle the apples with the sugar and cook until caramelised. Add the cider vinegar, gently stir and let bubble until evaporated. Add the cider and allow to bubble for 1 minute. Remove from the heat; keep warm.

5 Meanwhile, heat the oil for shallow-frying in a frying pan, add the goat's cheese and fry for about 1-2 minutes each side, turning only once. The cheeses are ready when the couscous grains are lightly flecked golden brown – you should also be able to smell the cheese.

6 Divide the rest of the watercress between 4 serving plates and top with the apple slices. Pour over the apple and cider juices and top with a couscous-crusted goat's cheese. Using a teaspoon, drizzle some watercress oil around each plate, and finally add a few drops of balsamic vinegar. Serve at once.

Marinated Field Mushrooms with Warm Welsh Goat's Cheese and Basil Pesto

4 medium, even-sized field mushrooms, trimmed
30 ml (2 tbsp) olive oil
4 individual Welsh goat's cheeses

Marinade:
100 ml (3½ fl oz) extra-virgin olive oil
1 clove garlic, crushed
grated zest and juice of 1 lemon
25 ml (1 fl oz) balsamic vinegar
few parsley sprigs, leaves only – chopped
few rosemary sprigs, leaves only – chopped
6 chives, snipped

Pesto:
10 basil leaves
10 parsley leaves
2 cloves garlic
25 g (1 oz) pine nuts
120 ml (4 fl oz) extra-virgin olive oil
50 g (2 oz) Parmesan cheese, freshly grated
salt and freshly ground black pepper

1 For the marinade, mix all of the ingredients together in a shallow dish. Add the mushrooms, turn to coat with the mixture and leave to marinate for about 45 minutes.

2 To make the pesto, place all of the ingredients in a blender or food processor and work to a coarse paste.

3 When ready to serve, remove the mushrooms from the marinade, reserving the marinade. Heat the 30 ml (2 tbsp) olive oil in a frying pan, add the mushrooms and fry over a high heat for about 1 minute each side until golden brown. Spoon over the reserved marinade; keep warm.

4 Meanwhile, place the goat's cheeses on a baking sheet and place in a preheated oven at 190°C (375°F) mark 5 for approximately 1 minute to warm.

5 Place a goat's cheese in the centre of each serving plate, top with a mushroom and drizzle over the pesto to serve.

Main Courses

Thai Mixed Fish with Hot Banana Salsa

4 cod steaks (cut from the middle), each
  125-150 g (4-5 oz)
15 ml (1 tbsp) sesame oil
2 large cloves garlic, finely chopped
5 cm (2 inch) piece fresh root ginger, peeled
  and chopped
1 large onion, thinly sliced into rings
5 ml (1 tsp) cumin seeds
5 ml (1 tsp) coriander seeds
2.5 ml (½ tsp) turmeric
175 g (6 oz) cherry tomatoes
2 star anise, in pieces
2 red chillies, deseeded and sliced into long,
  thin strips
2 lemon grass stalks
grated zest of 1 lime or lemon
450 ml (¾ pint) coconut milk
  (approximately)
salt and freshly ground black pepper
5 ml (1 tsp) Thai fish sauce
30 ml (2 tbsp) lime or lemon juice
16 baby corn cobs
1 bunch coriander sprigs, stalks removed
16 mangetout
8 spring onions, diagonally sliced
16 mussels in shells, par-cooked until open
16 raw prawns in shell
8 squid, cleaned and sliced into rings

Hot Banana Salsa:
1 large banana, chopped
½ red pepper, diced
½ green pepper, sliced
1 jalapeño chilli, deseeded and chopped
2.5 ml (½ tsp) chopped fresh root ginger
2 spring onions, finely chopped
30 ml (2 tbsp) lime juice (approximately)
15 ml (1 tbsp) light brown sugar
  (approximately)
7.5 ml (½ tbsp) olive oil

To Serve:
Buttered Noodles (see page 106)

1 First prepare the banana salsa. Combine all of the ingredients in a bowl and gently mix together, seasoning with salt and pepper to taste. Correct the acidity if necessary by adding a little extra lime juice or sugar to taste. Cover and refrigerate until ready to serve.

2 Heat the sesame oil in a small pan, add the garlic, ginger and onion rings and fry over a moderate heat until softened; remove from the heat. Dry-fry the cumin and coriander seeds in another pan until they begin to release their aroma. Transfer to a mortar and finely grind with the pestle. Add the ground spices and turmeric to the onion and garlic mixture, return to the heat and fry for 1-2 minutes.

3 Transfer to a large shallow flameproof casserole dish or ovenproof sauté pan and add the fish steaks, cherry tomatoes, star anise, chillies, lemon grass, lime or lemon zest, coconut milk, salt, pepper, fish sauce and lime or lemon juice. Bring to a gentle simmer, then cover and cook in a preheated oven at 160°C (325°F) mark 3 for 15 minutes.

4 Meanwhile, steam or par-boil the baby corn for 2-3 minutes; they should still have a firm texture. Chop the coriander leaves, reserving some whole for garnish.

5 Add all the remaining ingredients to the casserole. Check the consistency of the sauce and add a little extra coconut milk if necessary. Re-cover and return to the oven for a further 10 minutes or until all the fish and vegetables are cooked through. Check the seasoning and serve at once, garnished with coriander leaves and accompanied by the banana salsa and noodles.

Monkfish and Mussels with Lemon Saffron Sauce

2 monkfish tails, skinned, boned and
   membranes removed
900 g (2 lb) mussels in shells
8 chives
40 g (1½ oz) unsalted butter, chilled and
   diced
4 shallots, finely chopped
large pinch of saffron strands
250 ml (8 fl oz) dry white wine
150 ml (¼ pint) double cream
lemon juice, to taste
salt and freshly ground black pepper
a little olive oil, for cooking

To Serve:
Timbales of Basmati and Wild Rice (see
   page 106)
stir-fried broccoli flavoured with sesame
   seeds

1 Cut the monkfish into 8 strips. Scrub the mussels thoroughly under cold running water, removing their beards and discarding any with damaged shells or ones which remain open when tapped sharply with the back of a knife. Blanch the chives in boiling water for a few seconds; drain and set aside for the garnish.

2 Melt 15 g (½ oz) of the butter in a large pan, add the shallots with the saffron, cover and sweat until soft. Add the wine and bring to the boil.

3 Toss in the mussels, cover and cook for about 3 minutes until the shells have just opened. Strain and reserve the liquor. Set aside 12 mussels for garnish; remove the rest from their shells, discarding any unopened ones.

4 Bring the reserved liquor to the boil and reduce to approximately 150 ml (¼ pint). Add the cream and heat through. Whisk in the remaining butter, a piece at a time, then flavour with lemon juice to taste. Season with salt and pepper; set aside.

5 Lightly oil a griddle or heavy-based frying pan with a little olive oil and heat until almost smoking. Add the monkfish and cook for 1 minute, turning to sear on all sides. Transfer to a baking tray and roast in a preheated oven at 200°C (400°F) mark 6 for 7-8 minutes.

6 In the meantime, gently heat the sauce through, then add the shelled mussels to warm through. Transfer the monkfish to warmed plates and surround with the mussels and a pool of sauce. Garnish with the chives and reserved mussels in shells. Serve at once, with the rice timbales and stir-fried broccoli with sesame seeds.

Fillets of Sole with Pesto on a Sweet Pepper Ratatouille, served with a Basil and Vermouth Sauce

12 small lemon sole fillets, skinned
120 ml (4 fl oz) fish stock
120 ml (4 fl oz) dry white wine

Pesto:
50 g (2 oz) basil leaves
40 g (1½ oz) pine nuts
40 g (1½ oz) Parmesan cheese, freshly grated
1 clove garlic, peeled
1.25 ml (¼ tsp) salt
90 ml (3 fl oz) olive oil

Sauce:
250 ml (8 fl oz) fish stock
120 ml (4 fl oz) dry vermouth
150 ml (¼ pint) double cream
50 g (2 oz) unsalted butter, in pieces
10 basil leaves, shredded

Ratatouille:
25 g (1 oz) butter
1 shallot, finely diced
1 red pepper, cored, deseeded and diced
1 green pepper, cored, deseeded and diced

To Garnish:
1 carrot, cut into julienne
1 leek (white part only), cut into julienne
oil, for frying

1 First make the pesto. Place all the ingredients, except the oil, in a food processor or blender and work until smooth. With the motor running, add the oil in a thin stream through the feeder tube, processing until combined.

2 Lay the sole fillets on a clean surface, skinned-side up. Spread with the pesto and roll up the sole fillets to enclose the filling.

3 Pour the fish stock and wine into an ovenproof dish and heat until the liquid starts to tremble. Lay the rolled fillets in the dish, cover with buttered foil and cook in a preheated oven at 200°C (400°F) mark 6 for 10 minutes.

4 Meanwhile, make the sauce. Pour the fish stock and vermouth into a pan, bring to the boil and reduce by half. Add the cream and continue to reduce until the sauce starts to thicken. Take off the heat and whisk in the butter, a piece at a time. Stir in the shredded basil and check the seasoning.

5 For the pepper ratatouille, melt the butter in a pan, add the shallot and sweat gently until just tender. Add the diced peppers and sauté for 1 minute.

6 To prepare the garnish, heat a 4 cm (1½ inch) depth of oil in a pan and deep-fry the carrot and leek julienne until crisp and golden; drain on kitchen paper.

7 To serve, arrange a bed of peppers in the centre of each warmed serving plate and place the sole fillets on top. Pour the sauce around the peppers. Place a mound of deep-fried carrot and leek strips on top of the fish and serve at once.

Pan-fried Sea Bass with a Crisp Potato Topping on a bed of Leeks with a Red Pepper Sauce

4 sea bass fillets, each about 150 g (5 oz), skinned
olive oil, for frying

Potato Topping:
2 medium potatoes, peeled
salt and freshly ground black pepper
1 egg yolk, beaten

Red Pepper Sauce:
45 ml (3 tbsp) olive oil
3 red peppers, cored, deseeded and quartered
2 shallots, finely chopped
2 basil leaves
2 cloves garlic, peeled
30 ml (1 fl oz) white wine vinegar
200 ml (7 fl oz) dry vermouth
300 ml (½ pint) vegetable stock
150 ml (¼ pint) water
25 g (1 oz) butter, in pieces
squeeze of lemon juice

For the Leeks:
2 large leeks, trimmed
25 g (1 oz) butter

1 First make the sauce. Heat the olive oil in a frying pan. Add the peppers, shallots, basil and garlic and fry for about 5 minutes until soft, but not browned. Add the wine vinegar and cook for a further 2 minutes. Then add the vermouth, increase the heat and reduce until syrupy. Add the stock and water and bring to the boil. Simmer, uncovered, for 20 minutes. Discard the garlic. Purée the sauce in a blender or food processor, then pass through a muslin-lined sieve into a clean pan.

2 To prepare the potato topping, coarsely grate the potatoes, wrap in a clean tea-towel and wring out as much moisture as possible; do not rinse. Turn into a bowl, season with salt and pepper and bind with the egg yolk.

3 Press a handful of the potato mixture on top of each sea bass fillet to make a crust, about 5 mm (¼ inch) thick.

4 Slice the leeks into 5 cm (2 inch) julienne. Place in a sieve and pour over a freshly boiled kettle of water. Leave to drain, then pat dry.

5 To cook the sea bass, heat a little olive oil in a large heavy-based frying pan. Carefully place the fish in the pan, potato-side down. Cook for 4-5 minutes, until golden brown. Carefully turn the fillets over and cook for a further 3-4 minutes.

6 Meanwhile stir-fry the leeks in the butter for about 1 minute; they should retain some bite.

7 Meanwhile, reheat the sauce and reduce a little further if required. Whisk in the butter and lemon juice and season with salt and pepper to taste. To serve, pile the leeks onto each warmed serving plate and carefully position a fish fillet on top. Surround with the sauce and serve at once.

Steamed Fillets of Sea Bass with a Pernod Sauce

2 small sea bass, filleted (bones reserved)
15 g (½ oz) unsalted butter
1 shallot, finely chopped
30 ml (1 fl oz) Pernod
120 ml (4 fl oz) dry white wine
120 ml (4 fl oz) fish stock
150 ml (¼ pint) double cream
salt and freshly ground white pepper
few tarragon leaves

To Serve:
Fennel, Chervil and Tomato Casserole
   (see page 93)
Saffron Rice (see page 105)

1 Heat the butter in a pan, add the shallot and sweat for 2 minutes. Add the Pernod and flame. Once the flames have died down, add the white wine and reduce by half, then add the fish stock and reduce by half again. Stir in the cream and reduce to the desired consistency. Season with salt and pepper to taste; keep warm.

2 Cut each sea bass fillet diagonally in two. Season lightly and wrap each one in a piece of non-stick baking parchment, sealing the parcel tightly. Place in a steamer over boiling water and steam for 2-3 minutes until opaque.

3 Just before the fish will be ready, snip the tarragon leaves into the sauce.

4 To serve, unwrap the sea bass and place on warmed serving plates on top of the fennel. Spoon the sauce around the fish and serve at once, with the saffron rice.

Note: Chop up the fish bones and use to make the fish stock for the sauce.

Sautéed Red Snapper with Vegetable Tempura, Thai King Prawn Cake and a Ginger Soy Sesame Dressing

4 red snapper fillets, each about 175 g (6 oz)
squeeze of lime juice
salt and freshly ground black pepper
plain flour, for dusting
25 ml (1 fl oz) sesame oil

Prawn Cakes:
350 g (12 oz) raw king prawns, peeled and
   deveined
50 g (2 oz) coriander leaves, chopped
50 g (2 oz) chilli paste
50 g (2 oz) pickled ginger, plus a little of the
   juice
50 g (2 oz) lemon grass purée
25 g (1 oz) sesame seeds
5 ml (1 tsp) lime juice
finely grated zest of 1 lime
25 g (1 oz) red or green chillies, deseeded
50 g (2 oz) mint leaves, chopped
pinch of old bay seasoning
knob of butter
60 ml (2 fl oz) sesame oil
25 g (1 oz) spring onions, chopped
25 g (1 oz) peanuts, chopped
plain flour, for dusting
25 ml (1 fl oz) oil, for frying

Vegetable Tempura:
1 carrot, peeled
1 red pepper, halved, cored and deseeded
1 courgette, trimmed
1 leek, trimmed
1 sweet potato, peeled
50 g (2 oz) plain flour
150 ml (¼ pint) water
oil, for deep-frying

Dressing:

1 egg white
30 ml (2 tbsp) light soy sauce
5 ml (1 tsp) French mustard
25 ml (1 fl oz) sesame oil
50 ml (2 fl oz) sunflower oil
juice of 1 lime
25 g (1 oz) sesame seeds
15 ml (1 tbsp) pickled ginger juice
25 g (1 oz) chillies, deseeded and diced
100 g (4 oz) coriander leaves, chopped
4 ml (⅓ tsp) wasabi powder

1 First make the prawn cakes. Place half of the prawns in a blender or food processor with all of the rest of the ingredients (except the flour and oil for frying). Work until smooth, then add the remaining prawns and process briefly, keeping the added prawns quite chunky. Divide the mixture into 4 equal portions and shape each into a flat, round cake, about 1 cm (½ inch) thick. Cover and refrigerate.

2 For the tempura, cut the vegetables into julienne strips, mix together in a bowl and set aside. To make the batter, sift the flour into a bowl, add a pinch of salt and gradually mix in the water to form a smooth, thin batter; set aside.

3 To make the dressing, lightly whisk the egg white, soy sauce and mustard together in a bowl. Gradually add the oils, whisking to emulsify. Add the lime juice, sesame seeds, ginger juice, diced chillies, coriander and wasabi powder. Season with salt and pepper to taste. Leave to stand.

4 Sprinkle the red snapper fillets with lime juice and season with salt and pepper. Dust lightly with flour, shaking off excess.

5 Heat the sesame oil in a frying pan, add the fish fillets and pan-fry, skin-side down

for 30 seconds - 1 minute until crisp and golden brown. Transfer to a warmed ovenproof dish and place in a preheated oven at 190°C (375°F) mark 5 for 2-3 minutes to finish cooking.

6 Meanwhile, cook the prawn cakes. Heat the oil in a frying pan. Dust the prawn cakes lightly with flour, add to the hot oil and fry for about 30 seconds-1 minute each side, until crisp and golden. Transfer to a warmed ovenproof dish and place in the oven (with the red snapper) for 2-3 minutes.

7 In the meantime, cook the tempura in batches. Heat the oil for deep-frying in a suitable pan. Dip the vegetables into the batter to coat, then deep-fry in the hot oil for 1-2 minutes until crisp and golden. Drain on kitchen paper and season with salt and pepper.

8 To serve, spoon a mound of vegetable tempura onto one side of each warmed serving plate and place a prawn cake on top. Place a red snapper fillet on each plate and drizzle the dressing around the edge. Serve at once.

Seared Fillet of Salmon on Sautéed Fennel, Spinach and New Potatoes with Pastis

600 g (1 lb 4 oz) middle-cut salmon fillet
    (with skin), preferably wild salmon
1 fennel bulb, trimmed
500 ml (16 fl oz) well-flavoured reduced
    fish stock
250 ml (8 fl oz) dry white wine
1 star anise
15 ml (1 tbsp) Pastis, Pernod or Ricard
15 ml (1 tbsp) crème fraîche
salt and freshly ground black pepper
500 g (1 lb 2 oz) baby new potatoes
few knobs of unsalted butter
500 g (1 lb 2 oz) spinach leaves, stalks
    removed
splash of groundnut oil, for frying

1 Cut the salmon into 4 equal portions and remove any small residual bones with tweezers. Cut the fennel bulbs lengthwise into 12 equal slices, discarding the tough inner core.

2 Pour the fish stock and white wine into a pan, bring to the boil over a high heat and boil rapidly until reduced by about one third. Turn the heat down, add the star anise, Pastis and fennel pieces and poach for about 30 minutes, or until tender. Using a slotted spoon transfer the fennel to a dish, cover and keep warm. Increase the heat and boil rapidly again until the liquor is reduced to about 250 ml (8 fl oz) – and is thickened and intensified in flavour. Strain into a small saucepan and whisk in the crème fraîche. Taste and add seasoning if necessary.

3 Cook the new potatoes in boiling salted water until almost tender. Drain, return to the pan and add a knob of butter. Cover and cook over a low heat, shaking the pan from time to time to ensure the potatoes brown all over; keep hot.

4 Meanwhile, cook the spinach with just the water clinging to the leaves after washing in a pan over a medium heat, turning until wilted, but not soft. Remove from the heat, add a small piece of butter and season with salt and pepper. Keep warm.

5 Preheat a non-stick frying pan over a medium heat, then add a splash of groundnut oil and a knob of butter. When the butter starts to sizzle, lay the salmon fillets in the pan, skin-side down. Cook for approximately 2 minutes, or until the skin is brown and crispy. Turn over and cook the other side for no more than 1 minute, this will leave the fish slightly underdone in the centre – don't overcook it or it will become tough and dry.

6 Remove the salmon fillets from the pan and place in a warm dish, cover and leave to rest for 5 minutes; during this time the fish will finish cooking.

7 In the meantime, preheat a cast-iron griddle or heavy-based frying pan over a high heat and brush with a little groundnut oil. When it begins to smoke, add the pieces of fennel. Cook, undisturbed, for about 2 minutes until the underside is charred, then flip over and cook the other side for 1-2 minutes.

8 To assemble the dish, arrange three segments of fennel in the middle of each warmed serving plate, fanning them out in a circle. Place three small mounds of spinach in between the fennel and scatter over a handful of new potatoes. Position a salmon fillet, skin-side up, on top of each pile of vegetables. Spoon the sauce around the fish and vegetables. Serve at once.

Fillet of Oak-smoked Haddock with a Herb Crust

2 large oak-smoked haddock fillets, each
about 300-350 g (10-12 oz), skinned
(see note)

Crust:
4 thick slices of white bread, crusts removed
2 shallots, finely chopped
50 g (2 oz) unsalted butter
30 ml (2 tbsp) chopped flat-leaf parsley
30 ml (2 tbsp) chopped mixed herbs (sage,
coriander, dill and thyme)
salt and freshly ground black pepper

To Serve:
Pan-fried Potato and Celeriac Pancakes
(see page 100)
Julienne of Red Onion and Red Pepper
(see page 96)
Lemon and Mustard-dressed Leaves (see
page 90)

1 To prepare the crust, work the bread to fine crumbs, using a blender or food processor; set aside. Sauté the chopped shallots in the butter for 2 minutes until softened. Take off the heat and mix in the herbs and breadcrumbs to make a paste. Season with salt and pepper to taste.

2 Remove any residual bones from the fish fillets with tweezers and cut each fillet in half to give 4 portions.

3 Place the haddock fillets on a baking tray and press the crust evenly on top, to a depth of 1 cm (½ inch). Bake in a preheated oven at 190°C (375°F) mark 5 for 5 minutes, then cook under a preheated grill for a further 5 minutes until the crust is golden and the haddock flesh is pale cream in colour.

4 To serve, lay a pancake on each warmed serving plate. Cover with the julienne of red onion and red pepper and surround with the lemon and mustard dressed leaves. Top with the haddock fillet, spooning a little of the reserved salad dressing around the fish. Serve at once.

Note: If possible, get your fishmonger to skin the haddock fillets for you. Use undyed smoked haddock.

Smoked Haddock with a Grainy Mustard Sauce, Potato Salad, Spinach and Deep-fried Leeks

4 smoked haddock fillets, each about 175 g
  (6 oz)
50 g (2 oz) butter
2 shallots, diced
250 ml (8 fl oz) white wine
250 ml (8 fl oz) dry vermouth
300 ml (½ pint) vegetable stock
150 ml (¼ pint) double cream
2 rashers streaky bacon, derinded
15 ml (1 tbsp) chopped chives, or to taste
5-10 ml (1-2 tsp) wholegrain mustard, or to
  taste
225 g (8 oz) new potatoes
salt and freshly ground black pepper
10 ml (2 tsp) olive oil
5 ml (1 tsp) white wine vinegar
2 leeks, trimmed
groundnut oil, for deep-frying
600 ml (1 pint) milk
225 g (8 oz) spinach leaves, stalks removed
freshly grated nutmeg

1 Trim the fish fillets if necessary and remove any residual bones with tweezers.

2 To make the sauce, melt 25 g (1 oz) of the butter in a medium saucepan, add the shallots and sweat until soft. Add the wine, bring to the boil and reduce until almost completely evaporated. Add the vermouth and reduce again almost totally. Add the stock and reduce by about three-quarters. Finally add the cream and reduce to a good sauce consistency.

3 In the meantime, cut the bacon into lardons and fry in a heavy-based pan in their own fat until nearly crisp. Drain off the fat and add the lardons to the sauce with two thirds of the chives and mustard to taste; keep warm.

4 In the meantime, cook the new potatoes in boiling salted water until just tender; drain. Whilst still hot slice the potatoes and toss in the olive oil and vinegar. Season with salt and pepper to taste. Allow to cool slightly, then toss with the remaining chives.

5 Split the leeks in half lengthwise and slice finely into julienne strips. Pat dry with kitchen paper if necessary. Heat the oil for deep-frying in a suitable pan and deep-fry the leeks in batches for 15-30 seconds until crisp and golden brown. Drain on kitchen paper, season with salt and allow to cool.

6 Bring the milk to simmering point in a large shallow pan. Lay the haddock fillets in the pan and poach gently for about 5 minutes, until just cooked.

7 Meanwhile, heat the remaining 25 g (1 oz) butter in a large pan, add the spinach with just the water clinging to the leaves after washing and cook, uncovered, over a moderate heat until just wilted. Drain off the liquid, then season with salt, pepper and nutmeg to taste.

8 To serve, place a small round of warm potato salad in the centre of each warmed serving plate and surround with balls of spinach. Position the haddock on top of the potato, then sprinkle on some deep-fried leeks. Pour the sauce around the spinach and serve at once.

Fish Parcels

Ask your fishmonger for the bones and heads from the fish, which you will need to make the stock.

4 hake, turbot or sea bream fillets, each
about 175 g (6 oz)
salt and freshly ground black pepper
1 egg white, lightly beaten

Marinade:
30 ml (2 tbsp) olive oil
3-4 rosemary sprigs
4 basil leaves
4 tomatoes, chopped

Stock:
2 shallots, chopped
1 clove garlic, crushed
reserved fish bones and heads
450 ml (¾ pint) water
½ glass dry white wine
½ bay leaf
30 ml (2 tbsp) olive oil
squeeze of lemon juice

For the Parcels:
1 small fennel bulb, trimmed
1 courgette, trimmed
2 tomatoes, skinned, seeded and cut into
strips

To Serve:
Red Pesto Mashed Potato (see page 103)
Butter Beans and Leeks in Noilly Prat (see
page 94)

1 Lay the fish fillets in a shallow dish. Add the marinade ingredients and seasoning. Turn the fish to coat with the mixture and leave to marinate at cool room temperature for 1 hour.

2 To make the stock, put the shallots, garlic, fish bones and heads into a large saucepan. Add the water, wine, bay leaf and seasoning. Bring to the boil and simmer for approximately 10 minutes. Pass through a fine sieve and return to the pan. Bring to the boil and reduce to 150 ml (¼ pint). Add the olive oil and lemon juice to taste. Stir well and check the seasoning. Leave to cool.

3 Slice the fennel and courgette. Add the fennel to a pan of boiling salted water and boil for 2-3 minutes; add the courgette and boil for a further 1 minute. Drain, refresh in cold water and drain thoroughly.

4 Cut four circles of greaseproof paper, 35 cm (14 inches) in diameter and brush the edges with egg white. Arrange a layer of fennel, courgette and tomato on one half of each circle and moisten each with 15 ml (1 tbsp) of the reduced fish stock.

5 Lay a fish fillet on each bed of vegetables and top with the remaining vegetables; moisten with a little stock. Fold the other half of the paper over to form semi-circular parcels. Press the edges together and fold them to seal.

6 Place on a lightly oiled large baking sheet and bake in a preheated oven at 230°C (450°F) mark 8 for 8-10 minutes until the fish is just cooked through. Serve in the parcels, with the accompaniments.

Corn-fed Chicken Breast with Mole Sauce

4 corn-fed chicken breasts
salt and freshly ground black pepper

Sauce:
1 onion, chopped
2 cloves garlic, crushed
1 fresh or 2-3 dried chillies
10 ml (2 tsp) mole spice mix (see below)
30 ml (2 tbsp) tomato paste
juice of 1 lime
30 ml (2 tbsp) olive oil
400 g (14 oz) can plum tomatoes
300 ml (½ pint) chicken stock
15 g (½ oz) dark chocolate

To Serve:
Arroz Blanco (see page 105)
Salsa Stacks (see page 88)

1 To make the sauce, put the onion, garlic, chillies, spice mix, tomato paste and lime juice in a food processor and work to a thick paste, adding a little water to mix, if necessary.

2 Heat the oil in a saucepan. Add the spice paste mixture and fry gently for about 5 minutes until the spices release their aromas. Add the tomatoes with their juice and chicken stock. Bring to the boil and simmer, uncovered, for 20-30 minutes. Pass the mixture through a chinois (or other fine-meshed strainer) into a clean pan.

3 Preheat a ridged cast-iron griddle or heavy-based ovenproof frying pan until very hot. Season the chicken with pepper, place in the pan skin-side down and quickly sear until the skin is golden. Turn the chicken breasts over and transfer the pan to a preheated oven at 200°C (400°F) mark 6. Cook for about 20 minutes until tender.

4 Meanwhile, simmer the mole sauce gently for about 5 minutes to reduce slightly. Stir in the chocolate and simmer for about 5 minutes until you have a rich glossy sauce. Check the seasoning.

5 Allow the chicken to rest for a couple of minutes after cooking. To serve, pour the mole sauce onto the warmed serving plates and top with the chicken. Serve at once, with the arroz blanco and a salsa stack.

Mole Spice Mix: For this you will need: 25 g (1 oz) black peppercorns; 15 g (½ oz) cinnamon stick; 15 g (½ oz) star anise; 15 g (½ oz) cumin seeds; 5 ml (1 tsp) allspice berries; 15 g (½ oz) cloves. Grind the spices to a powder and store in an airtight jar.

Boned Stuffed Chicken

For this recipe you will need a boned whole chicken. Either ask your poulterer or butcher to bone the chicken for you or, if doing it yourself, make sure you choose a bird with a skin which is intact. You will need the bones to make the stock.

1.8 kg (4 lb) oven-ready chicken, boned
  (including the legs and wings)
50 g (2 oz) butter, melted

Stock:
reserved chicken bones
1 carrot, chopped
1 onion, quartered
1 bouquet garni (parsley, thyme, bay leaf)
6 white peppercorns
1.2 litres (2 pints) water

Stuffing:
15 g (1 oz) butter
1 small onion, finely chopped
225 g (8 oz) sausagemeat
30 ml (2 tbsp) fresh white breadcrumbs
1 small apple, peeled and chopped
pinch of chopped sage
1 egg
salt and freshly ground black pepper

To Serve:
thyme sprigs, to garnish
Potato Purée (see page 102)
Buttered Cabbage (see page 95)
Glazed Onions (see page 96)

1 Prepare the stock in advance. Put all of the ingredients in a saucepan, bring to the boil, then simmer, uncovered, for about 2 hours. Strain through a fine sieve into a clean pan, then reduce over a moderate heat to about 300 ml (½ pint). Set aside.

2 To make the stuffing, melt the butter in a pan, add the onion, cover and sweat gently until softened. Take off the heat. Mix the rest of the stuffing ingredients together in a bowl, then add the softened onion and beat well.

3 Lay the chicken, flesh-side uppermost, on a clean surface and spread the stuffing down the centre. Bring the sides of the chicken up over the stuffing and wrap over to enclose; tie at 2 or 3 intervals to secure. Wrap the chicken in a piece of muslin saturated with the melted butter. Tie the ends with string – to resemble a cracker.

4 Place the chicken on a rack over a roasting tin and roast in a preheated oven at 200°C (400°F) mark 6 for 1¼-1½ hours or until tender and the juices run clear when the chicken is pierced with a skewer.

5 Transfer the chicken to a warmed dish and leave to rest in a warm place for a few minutes. Skim off the fat from the juices in the roasting tin, then add the reduced stock and heat until bubbling, stirring to incorporate the meat juices. Check the seasoning and strain into a warmed sauceboat.

6 Carve the meat into slices and serve garnished with thyme and accompanied by the sauce, potato purée, buttered cabbage and glazed onions.

Breast of Guinea Fowl stuffed with a Rosemary-scented Mousseline

2 oven-ready guinea fowl
20 ml (4 tsp) chopped rosemary leaves
30 ml (2 tbsp) cream
1 small egg white (size 4 or 5)
1 small clove garlic
salt and freshly ground black pepper
about 8 spinach leaves, depending on size,
    stalks removed

Stock:
2 carrots, peeled
2 onions, peeled
2 celery sticks
handful of flavourful mushroom skins
2 rosemary sprigs
125 ml (4 fl oz) red wine
knob of butter

Plum Confit:
10-12 plums, stoned and roughly chopped
50 g (2 oz) sugar
200 ml (7 fl oz) red wine (approximately)
15 ml (1 tbsp) red wine vinegar
grated zest and juice of 1 small orange

To Serve:
Caramelised Fennel (see page 94)
Potato and Spinach Galettes (see page 99)

1 Carefully remove the breasts from the guinea fowl, reserving the skin, and set aside. Remove the thigh meat and chop roughly for the mousseline. Reserve the carcasses for the stock.

2 For the mousseline, put the thigh meat in a food processor and blend for a few seconds. Add the rosemary, cream, egg white, garlic and seasoning to taste. Blend briefly to form a mousseline. Transfer to a bowl, cover and refrigerate until needed.

3 Cook the whole spinach leaves in a pan with just the water clinging to the leaves after washing for about 30 seconds until just wilted. Drain and pat dry with kitchen paper.

4 Cut a pocket in the side of each guinea fowl breast. Press open and line with the wilted spinach leaves. Stuff with the mousseline and sew up the opening to form a 'sausage' shape.

5 To make the stock, joint the remaining guinea fowl carcasses and place in a roasting tin with the carrots, onions and celery. Cook in a preheated oven at 180°C (350°F) mark 4 for 30 minutes until the juices begin to run. Transfer the carcasses and vegetables to a large saucepan, add the mushroom skins and rosemary sprigs and barely cover with water. Slowly bring to the boil, skim the surface and simmer for approximately 1 hour.

6 Meanwhile, prepare the confit. Place all the ingredients in a small pan and slowly bring to a gentle simmer. Stir and simmer gently, uncovered, for approximately 30-40 minutes until the mixture is quite thick; keep warm.

7 Place the guinea fowl breasts in an ovenproof dish and cover with the reserved breast skins. Bake in a preheated oven at 190°C (375°F) mark 5 for 20-25 minutes until just cooked through. Transfer the guinea fowl to a warm dish and leave to rest in a warm place for 5 minutes.

8 Meanwhile, strain the stock and pour about 250 ml (8 fl oz) into the roasting tin, stirring to scrape up the sediment. Let bubble until reduced by half, then add the wine and reduce again to a syrupy consistency. Whisk in the knob of butter and season with salt and pepper to taste, the sauce should be thick enough to coat

the back of the spoon; strain through a fine sieve into a clean pan; reheat gently.

9 Discard the skins from the guinea fowl breasts and remove the trussing thread. Cut each breast into thin slices and arrange on a bed of caramelised fennel on warmed serving plates. Serve with the plum confit, sauce and potato and spinach galettes.

Braised Guinea Fowl with Prosciutto, Sage and Puy Lentils

4 guinea fowl breasts, with skin
18 sage leaves
8 slices of prosciutto (preferably San Daniele)
175 g (6 oz) Puy lentils
25 g (1 oz) butter
1 carrot, chopped
1 small onion, chopped
1 celery stick, chopped
300 ml (½ pint) dry white wine
60 ml (2 fl oz) Marsala
450 ml (¾ pint) chicken stock
30 ml (2 tbsp) chopped parsley

To Serve:
buttered savoy cabbage
Neeps and Tatties (see page 99)

1 Carefully loosen the skin from the guinea fowl breasts, keeping it attached along one side to form a pocket. Insert a slice of prosciutto into each pocket, trimming to fit as necessary; reserve the trimmings. Add 3 sage leaves to each pocket too. Pull the skin back into position and secure with a wooden cocktail stick, inserted lengthwise.

2 Put the lentils in a saucepan, add water to cover and bring to the boil. Lower the heat, cover and simmer for 20-30 minutes until tender; drain.

3 Chop the remaining prosciutto. Heat the butter in a large heavy-based frying pan, add the chopped carrot, onion, celery and prosciutto and fry for 3-4 minutes until beginning to colour. Move to the side of the pan.

4 Add the guinea fowl breasts to the pan, skin-side down and fry for a few minutes until nicely browned; remove from the pan.

5 Add the white wine and Marsala to the pan. Bring to the boil and reduce until syrupy. Chop the remaining sage leaves and add to the pan, along with the chicken stock. Bring to a simmer.

6 Return the guinea fowl breasts to the pan and poach for 10-20 minutes, depending on size, until just cooked. Lift the guinea fowl out of the pan and place in a warm dish; leave to rest in a warm place. Meanwhile, reduce the sauce by half, then add the lentils and parsley and simmer for a further 5 minutes.

7 To serve, cut the guinea fowl breasts into thick slices on the diagonal. Place a mound of buttered cabbage on each warmed serving plate and fan out the guinea fowl slices on top. Surround with the lentils and sauce. Serve at once, with the buttered cabbage, neeps and tatties.

Poached Breast of Guinea Fowl with a Sour Cream Sauce and Wild Mushrooms

15 g (½ oz) dried wild mushrooms
2 guinea fowl
600 ml (1 pint) concentrated chicken or
    guinea fowl stock
30 g (2 oz) fresh wild mushrooms, sliced
butter, for frying

Sauce:
25 g (1 oz) butter
50 g (2 oz) shallots, chopped
100 ml (3½ fl oz) dry white wine
275 ml (9 fl oz) soured cream
squeeze of lemon juice
salt and freshly ground black pepper

To Serve:
Truffled Potatoes (see page 103)
sautéed asparagus

1 Put the dried mushrooms in a bowl, pour on boiling water to cover and leave to soak for 30 minutes.

2 Meanwhile, remove and discard the legs and wings from the guinea fowl and the lower part of the carcass: you should be left with both portions of breast meat still attached to the breast bone and rib cage.

3 Bring the stock to the boil in a large pan. Add the birds and sufficient water to cover them. Poach for 10-12 minutes until cooked through. Drain and cool; discard the liquid.

4 Once the meat is cool enough to handle, slip off the skin and carefully remove the guinea fowl breasts from the bone.

5 Drain the dried mushrooms, reserving the liquid.

6 To make the sauce, melt the butter in a pan, add the shallots and sweat gently until softened but not coloured. Add the wine, bring to the boil and reduce until you are left with a film of liquid in the bottom of the pan. Add the soured cream and simmer for 5 minutes. Thin the sauce to a pouring consistency with the reserved mushroom liquid. Add a squeeze of lemon juice to enhance the flavour and season with salt and pepper to taste; keep warm over a low heat; do not allow to boil.

7 Heat a knob of butter in a frying pan and quickly sauté the dried and fresh mushrooms together for a few minutes. Remove with a slotted spoon; keep warm.

8 Add a little more butter to the frying pan and sauté the guinea fowl breasts quickly to colour and warm through. Strain the sauce through a sieve.

9 To serve, place a mound of potatoes in the centre of each warmed serving plate and flatten. Arrange some sautéed asparagus spears on top. Add some of the mushrooms, then top with the guinea fowl. Surround with the sauce and scatter over the remaining mushrooms. Serve at once.

Pan-fried Barbary Duck Breasts on Parsnip Mash and Savoy Cabbage with a Blackberry Game Sauce

Ask your poulterer or butcher for the duck carcasses and 2 wood pigeon carcasses, which you will need to make a well-flavoured stock.

4 Barbary duck breasts
salt and freshly ground black pepper

Sauce:
2 duck carcasses, chopped
2 wood pigeon carcasses, chopped
1 carrot
1 leek
1 celery stick
1 onion
few knobs of butter
350 ml (12 fl oz) full-bodied red wine
1 litre (1¾ pints) water
large handful of blackberries
3 bay leaves
12 sage leaves
1 rosemary sprig
3 egg whites

To Serve:
3 parsnips, peeled, cored and chopped
1 medium potato, peeled and cut into even-sized pieces
10 ml (2 tsp) crème fraîche
1 medium/small Savoy cabbage, cored and coarsely shredded

Parsnip Crisps:
2 parsnips, peeled
oil, for deep-frying
2 parsnips, peeled

To Garnish:
16 blackberries

1 Prick the skin of the duck breasts all over with a sharp knife (piercing the fat layer) and leave at room temperature, skin-side up, to dry.

2 To make the sauce, put the duck and pigeon carcasses into a large roasting tin and place in a preheated oven at 220°C (425°F) mark 7 for 20 minutes, turning once, until browned all over. Remove with a slotted spoon; set aside. Pour off the fat; reserve the carcasses and meat juices.

3 Meanwhile, chop the carrot, leek, celery and onion. Heat a knob of butter in a large pan, add the chopped vegetables, cover and sweat gently for about 15 minutes. Add the carcasses, red wine, reserved meat juices and water. Bring slowly to the boil and skim. Add the blackberries and herbs, reduce the heat and simmer gently for about 3 hours, skimming frequently.

4 Strain the stock through a conical sieve into a bowl, pressing to extract all liquid. Allow to cool, then remove all traces of fat from the surface. Return to the pan. To clarify the stock, turn up the heat and add the egg whites, stirring constantly until they coagulate, taking all the impurities to the surface with them. Simmer very gently for 1 minute, then skim off the mass of scum and discard. Strain through a muslin-lined sieve and return the now perfectly clear stock to the rinsed-out pan. Boil briskly until reduced to about 300 ml (½ pint); the sauce should be thickened and syrupy. Season to taste and set aside.

5 Place the parsnips in a roasting tin and bake in a preheated oven at 180°C (350°F) mark 4 for about 20 minutes, or until tender. Meanwhile, cook the potato in boiling salted water until tender; drain well. Mash the parsnip and potato together, then pass through a sieve into a warm bowl. Stir in the crème fraîche, season lightly and keep hot.

6 Steam the shredded cabbage for 5-10 minutes; it should still have some crunch. Drain well, season and keep hot.

7 To cook the duck breasts, place a large, non-stick frying pan over a high heat. Put the duck breasts in, skin-side down, and fry in their own fat for 5-8 minutes depending on size; pouring off the surplus duck fat from time to time. When the skin is brown and crispy, turn the breasts over and cook for a further 2-3 minutes. Remove from the pan, wrap in a double layer of foil and leave to rest in a warm place for at least 10 minutes.

8 Meanwhile, grease four 10 cm (4 inch) metal rings and place on a greased baking sheet. Spoon a portion of cabbage into each ring and gently press down, then place a slightly smaller portion of parsnip purée on top and level the surface. Keep hot in a warm oven.

9 To make the parsnip crisps, use a potato peeler or mandoline to pare off long strips from the parsnips. Heat the oil in a deep-fat fryer to about 175°C (350°F) and deep-fry the parsnip strips, a handful at a time, until crisp and golden brown. Remove with a slotted spoon and drain on kitchen paper.

10 To assemble, warm the sauce through, whisking in a few knobs of butter to thicken and add gloss. With the skin uppermost, thinly slice the duck breasts lengthwise and fan out on warmed serving plates. Release the parsnip and cabbage towers from the rings and place one at the point of each duck breast 'fan'. Arrange the parsnip crisps attractively on top. Spoon the sauce around the duck and garnish with blackberries. Serve at once.

Tea-smoked Duck with Courgette Tempura, Noodles, Baby Vegetables and a Coriander Salsa

4 duck breasts fillets (with skin)
3 star anise
4 small dried red chillies
2.5 ml (½ tsp) salt
45 ml (3 tbsp) soy sauce

Smoking Ingredients:
45 ml (3 tbsp) rice
45 ml (3 tbsp) earl grey or green gunpowder tea
45 ml (3 tbsp) sugar

Coriander Salsa:
1 large handful coriander sprigs, stalks removed
45 ml (3 tbsp) wine vinegar
30 ml (2 tbsp) dark soy sauce
30 ml (2 tbsp) olive oil
30 ml (2 tbsp) hazelnut oil
2.5 ml (½ tsp) ground coriander
15 ml (1 tbsp) caster sugar

Courgette Tempura:
75 g (3 oz) plain flour
25 g (1 oz) cornflour
1 egg
100 ml (3½ fl oz) iced water
3 medium courgettes, trimmed
flour, for dusting
oil, for deep-frying

To Serve:
1 packet dried egg noodles
handful of baby corn cobs
handful of baby carrots
handful of mangetout
salad leaves (eg rocket, celery leaves)
vinaigrette, for dressing
2.5-5 ml (½-1 tsp) soy sauce

1 First make the tempura batter. Sift the flour and cornflour together into a bowl. Add the egg, then gradually beat in the water to make a smooth, light batter. Cover and chill in the refrigerator for 1 hour.

2 Prick the skin of the duck breasts. Crush the star anise, chillies and salt together using a pestle and mortar, then dry-fry in a small heavy-based pan until they release their aroma. Allow to cool, then rub all over the duck breasts.

3 Lay the duck breasts, skin-side down, in a steamer (or in a covered wok – on a rack over boiling water) and par-cook for 5 minutes. Transfer the warm duck breasts to a shallow dish, drizzle over the soy sauce and leave to marinate for 30 minutes, turning occasionally.

4 In the meantime, prepare the coriander salsa. Place all the ingredients in a blender or food processor and whizz until finely chopped and evenly amalgamated. Turn into a bowl; set aside.

5 Double-line a wok with foil. Mix together the rice, tea and sugar and scatter over the base of the wok. Place the duck breasts on a raised plate over the smoking ingredients. Put the lid on the wok, sealing the edge tightly with strips of damp kitchen paper. Place over a high heat for 10 minutes, then take the wok off the heat but don't remove the lid. Leave to stand for 20 minutes.

6 Meanwhile, slice each courgette lengthwise into 6 strips. Heat the oil for deep-frying. Dust the courgette strips with flour, dip into the batter, then deep-fry in the hot oil until crisp and golden; keep hot.

7 Cook the egg noodles in boiling water according to the packet instructions. Blanch the baby corn, carrots and magetout separately in boiling water for 30 seconds - 1 minute until cooked but retaining some bite. Drain thoroughly, return to the pan and add the noodles and coriander salsa. Toss to mix and heat through.

8 To serve, toss the salad leaves in a little vinaigrtte to dress lightly and arrange on individual serving plates. Thinly slice the duck breasts on the diagonal, fan out on the bed of salad leaves and drizzle with a little soy sauce. Serve accompanied by the courgette tempura and coriander noodles and baby vegetables.

Breast of Duck with Lemon Grass, Coriander and Roast Squash

2 or 4 duck breast fillets, depending on size
salt and freshly ground black pepper

Jus:
300 ml (½ pint) reduced chicken stock
200 ml (7 fl oz) red wine
100 ml (3½ fl oz) Madeira
1 lemon grass stalk, chopped
few coriander sprigs
25 g (1 oz) unsalted butter, diced

Roast Squash:
2 gem squash
25 g (1 oz) salted butter

To Serve:
Carrot and Courgette Spaghetti (see page 91)
Gingered Potato and Parsnip Cakes (see page 101)

1 First prepare the jus. Put the stock and red wine in a pan, bring to the boil and reduce by half. Add the Madeira and reduce by a quarter, then add the lemon grass and boil for 2 minutes. Add the coriander, take off the heat and allow to infuse for 1 minute. Strain through a fine sieve, check the seasoning and set aside.

2 To prepare the squash, halve, deseed and scoop the flesh into balls, using a melon baller; you should make about 30 balls. Place in a roasting tin. Melt the salted butter and pour over the squash, coating each ball. Roast in a preheated oven at 220°C (425°F) mark 7, for 15 minutes.

3 Meanwhile cook the duck breasts. Rub the skin with salt. Preheat a heavy-based frying pan, add the duck breasts, skin-side down, and fry quickly for about 5 minutes until the skin is brown and crisp. Turn and briefly seal the other side, then place in a roasting tin, skin-side up. Cook in a preheated oven at 220°C (425°F) mark 7 for 10-15 minutes. Leave to rest in a warm place for 5 minutes. Meanwhile, reheat the sauce and whisk in the butter.

4 To serve, place a mound of carrot and courgette spaghetti in the middle of each warmed serving plate. Slice each duck breast thinly and arrange on top. Place the gingered potato cakes around the outside, alternating with the squash balls. Pour on a little jus and serve immediately.

Roast Spiced Barbary Duck with a Honey and Ginger Sauce

2 large Barbary duck breasts, each about
350 g (12 oz)
salt and freshly ground black pepper
pinch of cayenne pepper
100 ml (3½ fl oz) chicken stock
30 ml (2 tbsp) thin honey
30 ml (2 tbsp) mushroom soy sauce
15 ml (1 tbsp) grated fresh root ginger
pinch of chilli powder
15 ml (1 tbsp) tomato ketchup
30 ml (2 tbsp) rice wine, or medium
dry sherry
squeeze of lime juice

To Serve:
Roast Winter Vegetables (see page 97)
fondant or other potatoes (optional)

1 Trim the duck breasts and lightly score the skin with a sharp knife. Rub the skin with salt, then turn the breasts over and season the flesh with salt, pepper and a little cayenne pepper.

2 Preheat a cast-iron ovenproof frying pan. Lay the duck breasts in the pan, skin-side down, and cook for approximately 5 minutes until the skin is brown and crisp. Pour off the excess fat, turn the breasts over and cook for about 1 minute to seal the meat.

3 Turn the duck breasts again so they are skin-side up and transfer the pan to a preheated oven at 220°C (425°F) mark 7 for approximately 10 minutes, according to taste. Transfer the duck breasts to a warm dish, cover and leave to rest in a warm place for about 5 minutes.

4 Meanwhile, pour off any excess fat from the pan. Add all of the remaining ingredients to the pan, bring to the boil and boil for 2 minutes until the mixture thickens to a sauce consistency.

5 Slice the duck breasts thinly and arrange on warmed serving plates. Pour over a little of the sauce and serve at once with the roast vegetables, and potatoes if serving.

Roast Breast of Pheasant with Puy Lentils

For this recipe the pheasants should be well hung – for at least 10 days before preparation.

2 pheasants
oil, for frying

Stock:
pheasant legs and wings
1 litre (1¾ pints) water
1 celery stick, roughly chopped
1 leek, roughly chopped
1 onion, quartered
1 carrot, roughly chopped
1 thyme sprig
1 bay leaf
salt and freshly ground black pepper

For the Lentils:
100 g (3½ oz) Puy lentils
1 small onion
1 small carrot
½ celery stick
1 thyme sprig
few parsley stalks
1 bay leaf

To Finish Sauce:
200 ml (⅓ pint) red wine

To Serve:
Potato Rösti (see page 104)
Gratin of Celeriac and Parsnip (see page 99)
Chestnut Parcels (see below)
1 tomato, skinned, deseeded and diced

1 Prepare the stock in advance. Remove the legs and wings from the pheasant and place in a roasting tin. Roast in a preheated oven at 200°C (400°F) mark 6 for 20 minutes until dark golden brown in colour.

Drain off the fat and place in a saucepan. Pour on the water, bring to the boil and skim well. Add the celery, leek, onion, carrot, thyme, bay leaf and seasoning. Simmer for 4 hours, skimming regularly.

2 In the meantime, soak the lentils in cold water for 2 hours, then drain and place in a saucepan with the onion, carrot, celery and herbs. Cover with fresh cold water. Bring to the boil, lower the heat and simmer for 40 minutes or until tender.

3 To make the sauce, pass the stock through a fine sieve into a clean pan. Add the wine. Bring to the boil and reduce by two thirds until a sauce consistency is achieved. Check the seasoning.

4 Heat a little oil in a heavy-based oven-proof frying pan, add the pheasants and fry gently until evenly coloured. Transfer to a preheated oven at 230°C (450°F) mark 8 and cook for 10-12 minutes. Allow to rest in a warm place for about 5 minutes.

5 Drain the lentils thoroughly and adjust the seasoning.

6 To serve, spoon a mound of lentils onto the centre of each warmed serving plate and place a potato rösti on top. Carefully remove the breasts from the pheasant carcasses, slice and arrange on top of the röstis. Place a celeriac and parsnip gratin and a chestnut parcel on each plate. Spoon the sauce over the pheasant and around the lentils. Garnish with the diced tomato and serve at once.

Chestnut Parcels: Poach 8 chestnuts in a little salted water until tender. Drain, skin and dice. Blanch 4 cabbage leaves in boiling water until softened; drain. Divide the diced chestnuts between the cabbage leaves and fold to enclose. Keep warm until ready to serve.

Pheasant Breasts with Glazed Apple Slices, served with an Apple and Thyme Sauce

4 skinned, boneless pheasant breasts (see note)
salt and freshly ground black pepper
30 ml (2 tbsp) olive oil
200 ml (7 fl oz) dry white wine
25 g (1 oz) butter
300 ml (½ pint) game stock
2 red-skinned apples
30 ml (2 tbsp) Calvados
150 g (5 oz) crème fraîche
15 ml (1 tbsp) chopped thyme
20 ml (1½ tbsp) apple and thyme jelly
splash of cider vinegar (optional)
thyme sprigs, to garnish

To Serve:
Potato and Celeriac Julienne (see page 100)
Skirlie (see page 106)
Buttered Savoy Cabbage (see page 95)

1 Season the pheasant breasts with salt and pepper. Rub all over with olive oil, place in a shallow dish and sprinkle with a little of the white wine. Leave to marinate in a cool place for 30 minutes - 1 hour.

2 Melt half of the butter in a heavy-based frying pan. When hot, add the pheasant breasts and cook gently for about 4 minutes on each side. Using a slotted spoon, transfer the pheasant breasts to a roasting tin and sprinkle with a few spoonfuls of the game stock. Finish cooking in a preheated oven at 190°C (375°F) mark 5 for 10-15 minutes.

3 Meanwhile, add the remaining butter to the frying pan and heat. Halve, core and slice each apple into 8 wedges; do not peel. Add to the pan and sauté gently for about 5 minutes until softened. Remove from the pan; keep warm.

4 For the sauce, add the Calvados to the pan and let bubble until well reduced. Add the wine and reduce by half, then add the stock and reduce again by half. Stir in the crème fraîche, followed by the chopped thyme and apple jelly; bring to the boil. Season with salt and pepper to taste and sharpen with a splash of cider vinegar if necessary; keep warm.

5 To serve, slice the pheasant breasts diagonally, adding any juices to the sauce. Place a mound of potato and celeriac julienne on each warmed serving plate and arrange the pheasant slices, fanned out, on top. Arrange the apple slices on the plate to form a rosette. Garnish with thyme and pour on the sauce. Serve with the skirlie and buttered cabbage.

Note: Use the pheasant carcasses to make a well-flavoured stock for the sauce.

Pheasant with Madeira, Stuffed Cider Cabbage, Lentils and Parsnip Mash

2 pheasants
salt and freshly ground black pepper
25 g (1 oz) butter
4-6 rashers streaky bacon, halved

Stock:
25 g (1 oz) butter
1 carrot, diced
1 onion, diced
1 leek, diced
1 celery stick, diced
1 bay leaf
few black peppercorns

Sauce:
25 g (1 oz) butter
1 shallot, diced
½ bottle Madeira
1 thyme sprig (leaves only), chopped

For the Cabbage:
1 small Savoy cabbage
15 g (½ oz) duck fat
1 onion, sliced
2 rashers streaky bacon, derinded and diced
1 small eating apple, peeled, cored and diced
600 ml (1 pint) dry cider

For the Lentils:
15 g (½ oz) duck fat
1 onion, diced
1 carrot, diced
1 leek, diced
1 celery stick, diced
125 g (4 oz) lentils

Parsnip Mash:
350 g (12 oz) parsnips, peeled, cored and
*   roughly chopped*
knob of butter
freshly grated nutmeg, to taste

1 Remove the legs, wings and lower part of the carcass from each pheasant, leaving the breasts intact on the bone. Set the pheasant breasts aside.

2 To make the stock, chop the carcasses, legs and wings. Heat the butter in a large pan, add the diced vegetables and sweat until softened. Add the chopped pheasant legs, wings and carcasses, and brown with the vegetables. Pour on sufficient water to cover, then add the bay leaf and peppercorns. Bring to the boil, skim and simmer for 2-3 hours, skimming from time to time. Strain through a fine sieve.

3 To make the sauce, heat 15 g (½ oz) butter in a pan, add the shallot and sweat until softened. Add the Madeira and reduce by two thirds. Add 300 ml (½ pint) of the stock and reduce again by about two thirds. Check the seasoning.

4 To prepare the cabbage, remove the 4 outer leaves and set aside. Slice the rest of the cabbage, discarding the core. Heat the duck fat in a heavy-based pan, add the onion and sweat gently until softened. Add the bacon and sauté for a few minutes, then stir in the cabbage and apple. Pour in half of the cider, add seasoning and bring to a simmer. Cook for 30 minutes or until tender.

5 In the meantime, cook the lentils. Heat the duck fat in a saucepan, add the diced vegetables and sweat gently until softened. Add the lentils and cover with the remaining stock. Bring to the boil, lower heat and cook for 35 minutes or until tender. Drain thoroughly; keep warm.

6 Meanwhile, briefly blanch the reserved cabbage leaves in boiling water until pliable, drain and trim to 10-12 cm (5-6 inch) rounds, using a saucer as a guide.

Place a spoonful of the cooked cabbage mixture in the centre of each leaf, draw up the sides of the cabbage, twist together at the top and secure with a wooden cocktail stick. Heat the remaining cider in the base of the steamer. Place the cabbage parcels in the steamer and cook for 10-15 minutes until the outer leaf is soft.

7 Add the parsnips to a pan of cold salted water. Bring to the boil and simmer for about 10 minutes until tender. Drain thoroughly and pass through a mouli, or mash until smooth. Beat in the butter and season with salt, pepper and nutmeg to taste.

8 Season the pheasant breasts with salt and pepper, smear with butter and cover with the bacon rashers. Roast in a preheated oven at 180°C (350°F) mark 4 for about 20 minutes, or until tender. Cover and leave to rest in a warm place for 10 minutes. Meanwhile, reheat the sauce and stir in the chopped thyme.

9 To serve, remove the pheasant breasts from the bone, slice and arrange to one side of each warmed serving plate. Spoon some lentils opposite and place a cabbage ball on top. Shape quenelles of mashed parsnip and place on the plate. Pour on the sauce and serve immediately.

Venison with Sloe Gin

1 fillet of roe deer venison, about 600 g
    (1 lb 5 oz), cut into collops, 2 cm
    (¾ inch) thick
salt and coarsely ground black pepper
15 ml (1 tbsp) olive oil

Sauce:
15 ml (1 tbsp) gin
150 ml (¼ pint) beef or game stock
150 ml (¼ pint) sloe gin
10 ml (2 tsp) juniper berries, lightly crushed
25 g (1 oz) unsalted butter, in pieces
pinch of dry mustard

To Serve:
Clapshot (see page 95)
Deep-fried Leeks (see page 94)
Red Cabbage with Juniper (see page 95)

1 Season the venison with salt and pepper. Heat the olive oil in a heavy-based frying pan, add the venison and quickly brown over a high heat on all sides.

2 Transfer to a rack over a roasting tin and cook in a preheated oven at 200°C (400°F) mark 6 for about 5 minutes; the collops should still be pink in the middle. Transfer to a warmed dish, cover and leave to rest in a warm place while making the sauce.

3 To make the sauce, put the roasting tin over a moderate heat, pour in the gin and flame. When the flames die down, add the stock, sloe gin and juniper berries. Let bubble until reduced by half. Take off the heat and whisk in the butter, a piece at a time. Season with salt, pepper and mustard. Strain into a jug; keep warm.

4 To assemble, arrange the venison collops on a mound of clapshot and pile the leeks on top. Spoon the cabbage alongside. Pour on the sauce and serve immediately.

Pan-fried Pigeon Breasts

4 pigeons
60 ml (4 tbsp) olive oil
20 ml (4 tsp) Worcestershire sauce
20 ml (4 tsp) balsamic vinegar
20 ml (4 tsp) soy sauce
300 ml (½ pint) light red wine
16 mixed peppercorns
2 bay leaves
2 thyme sprigs
2 cloves garlic, crushed
2 shallots, chopped
15 ml (1 tbsp) redcurrant jelly
salt and freshly ground black pepper
50 g (2 oz) unsalted butter
knob of butter, for sauce

To Serve:
redcurrant sprigs, to garnish
Stir-fried Red Onions with Cabbage and
   Bacon (see page 96)
Pommes Mousseline with Chives (see page
   104)

1 To prepare the pigeons, remove the legs, then carefully cut the breasts from the carcasses, using a sharp knife.

2 For the marinade, combine the olive oil, Worcestershire sauce, balsamic vinegar, soy sauce, red wine, peppercorns, bay leaves, thyme, garlic and shallots in a shallow dish. Lay the pigeon breasts in the marinade and turn to coat. Cover and leave to marinate in the refrigerator for at least 12 hours, but preferably for 24 hours.

3 When ready to cook, remove the pigeon breasts from the marinade and pat dry with kitchen paper. Pour the marinade into a saucepan, bring to a simmer and reduce gently until thickened to a sauce consistency. Strain the sauce through a fine sieve and return to the pan. Add the redcurrant jelly and stir over a gentle heat until melted into the sauce. Check the seasoning; keep warm.

4 Melt the unsalted butter in a large heavy-based frying pan, add the pigeon breasts and fry gently for 5-10 minutes, depending on size. (If the pigeons are large you may need to cook them in 2 batches.) Turn off the heat, cover and leave to rest for 5-10 minutes.

5 To serve, stir a knob of butter into the sauce to give it a good sheen. Slice the pigeon breasts at an angle and arrange on warmed serving plates. Pour over the sauce and garnish with redcurrant sprigs. Serve at once, with the stir-fried onions, cabbage and bacon, and pommes mousseline.

Loin of Rabbit wrapped in Savoy Cabbage and Schufnudeln, served with a Madeira and Wild Mushroom Jus

2 boned saddles of rabbit (ie 4 loins and
  4 fillets)
4 Savoy cabbage leaves
30 ml (2 tbsp) oil

Sauce:
16 dried morels
8 dried ceps
¼ pint (150 ml) Madeira
½ pint (300 ml) rabbit stock

Schufnudeln:
625 g (1 lb 6 oz) potatoes
salt and freshly ground black pepper
50 g (2 oz) butter
1 egg yolk
75 g (3 oz) plain flour

To Assemble:
4 squares of crepinette (caul fat), each
  about 20 cm (8 inches)

To serve:
turnip purée

1 For the sauce, pre-soak the dried morels and ceps in the Madeira for 30 minutes.

2 To make the schufnudeln, peel the potatoes and cut into 1 cm (¾ inch) cubes. Cook in boiling salted water until soft. Drain and spread out on a baking sheet. Place in a preheated oven at 200°C (400°F) mark 6 for 5-15 minutes to dry out.

3 Remove the potatoes from the oven and spread out on a cold baking sheet. Dot with the butter and mash with a fork. Allow to cool. Turn the mashed potato onto a clean surface and gradually work in the egg yolk and flour, using a palette knife. Adjust the seasoning; set aside.

4 Blanch the cabbage leaves in boiling water for about 30 seconds until pliable; drain and pat dry on kitchen paper. Remove the tough centre stalks.

5 Season the rabbit. Heat the oil in a heavy-based ovenproof frying pan and quickly seal the rabbit on all sides. Lay the cabbage leaves flat on a clean surface and place a rabbit loin and a fillet on each one, positioning the fillet alongside the thin end of the loin. Roll up the cabbage leaves to enclose the rabbit and trim the ends as necessary.

6 On a clean surface well dusted with cornflour, spread out one quarter of the schufnudeln mixture with the palm of your hand until it is 5 mm (¼ inch) thick. Place a cabbage parcel on top and roll up in the potato mixture to completely enclose, forming a sausage shape; trim off any excess schufnudeln. Wrap each parcel in caul and twist the ends to secure; do not trim all excess caul away – you need to allow for some shrinkage.

7 Heat the oil remaining in the frying pan and brown the parcels on all sides. Transfer to a preheated oven at 220°C (425°F) mark 7 and cook for 20 minutes.

8 Meanwhile, make the sauce. Boil the rabbit stock to reduce by one third, then add the madeira and mushrooms. Reduce to the required consistency.

9 To assemble, cut each rabbit parcel into 1 cm (½ inch) thick slices and arrange on a warmed serving plate. Pour over the sauce and serve at once, with puréed turnip.

Note: Use the bones from the rabbit to make a well-flavoured stock for the sauce.

Roast Saddle of Lamb served on a bed of Spinach with a Tomato and Basil Sauce

2 boned loins of lamb, each about 250 g
  (9 oz), lean trimmings and bones
  reserved
30 ml (2 tbsp) sunflower oil
30 ml (2 tbsp) melted butter

Sauce:
5-6 lamb rib bones
75 g (3 oz) unsalted butter
50-75 g (2-3 oz) lamb trimmings
2 shallots, chopped
2 cloves garlic, crushed
1 bay leaf
1 thyme sprig
salt and freshly ground black pepper
2 ripe plum tomatoes, peeled
25 ml (1 fl oz) cognac
150 ml (¼ pint) elderberry wine (preferably
  homemade – see note)
400 ml (14 fl oz) chicken stock
200 ml (7 fl oz) water
8 large basil leaves, chopped
knob of butter (optional)

To Serve:
100 g (4 oz) spinach leaves, stalks removed
25 g (1 oz) butter
Potato Galettes (see page 102)
Glazed Shallots

1 First, make the sauce. Put the lamb bones in a roasting tin and roast in a preheated oven at 230°C (450°F) mark 8 for 20 minutes. Preheat a large heavy-based frying pan, add 25 g (1 oz) butter and, when foaming, add the lamb trimmings, shallots, garlic, bay leaf, thyme and pepper. Cook, turning frequently, until the ingredients are well browned. Halve and deseed the tomatoes; add the pulp and seeds to the pan, setting aside the tomato flesh for later use. Continue cooking until the mixture is dry.

2 Pour the cognac into the pan, then add the wine and reduce until all of the liquor has evaporated. Add the roasted lamb bones, stock and water and stir well. Bring to the boil and simmer over a low heat for about 50 minutes until reduced and thickened. Pass the sauce through a sieve and keep warm.

3 Season the lamb with salt and pepper. Heat a heavy-based ovenproof frying pan until hot, add the sunflower oil and 30 ml (2 tbsp) melted butter to the pan, then add the lamb and quickly brown all sides. Transfer to the preheated oven at 230°C (450°F) mark 8 and cook for 3-4 minutes or longer, depending on how pink you like your lamb. For 'well done' meat, allow up to 10 minutes.

4 Cover the lamb and leave to rest in a warm place for 10 minutes before carving. Meanwhile reheat the sauce if necessary and stir in the chopped tomato and basil. Whisk in a knob of butter to add gloss, if required.

5 Meanwhile, quickly cook the spinach in a large pan with 25 g (1 oz) butter until just wilted. Season with salt and pepper.

6 Divide the spinach between 4 warmed serving plates. Carve the lamb and arrange on top of the spinach. Serve at once with the sauce, potato galettes and glazed shallots.

Note: Homemade elderberry wine imparts a delicious sweetness to the sauce. If unobtainable, use a good full-bodied red wine instead.

Rosemary Lamb with a Redcurrant Sauce

2 racks of lamb, each with at least 6 cutlets,
    trimmed of all fat
few black peppercorns
2-3 rosemary sprigs, leaves only
10 ml (2 tsp) dried rosemary
450 ml (¾ pint) well-flavoured lamb stock
300 ml (½ pint) fruity red wine (Merlot or
    Shiraz)
1 red onion, thinly sliced
1 carrot, chopped
30 ml (2 tbsp) olive oil
15 ml (1 tbsp) redcurrant jelly
knob of butter
salt and freshly ground black pepper

To Serve:
Potato and Parsnip Cakes (see page 98)
Oven-baked Baby Vegetables (see page 89)

1 Crush the peppercorns with the fresh and dried rosemary, using a pestle and mortar. Rub this mixture over the lamb. Place in a dish and pour on the stock and about three quarters of the wine. Add the onion and carrot and leave to marinate for about 1 hour.

2 Lift the lamb out of the marinade. Strain the marinade, reserving the flavouring vegetables as well as the liquor.

3 Heat the olive oil in a heavy-based frying pan. Cut the lamb joints in half, add to the pan and seal for about 1 minute on each side. Transfer to a roasting tin and place in a preheated oven at 200°C (400°F) mark 6. Roast for approximately 12 minutes for medium-rare lamb, or longer if you prefer well-done meat.

4 Meanwhile, reheat the pan used to seal the lamb. Add the reserved vegetables and fry until lightly coloured. Add the remaining wine and let bubble until almost totally evaporated. Remove the vegetable mixture with a slotted spoon. Add the reserved marinade to the pan and boil until the sauce is well reduced and syrupy. Add the redcurrant jelly and a knob of butter to give the sauce a shine. Season with salt and pepper to taste.

5 Once the lamb is cooked, cover loosely with foil and leave to rest in a warm place for about 10 minutes.

6 To serve, slice the lamb into cutlets. Place a potato and parsnip cake on each warmed serving plate and arrange the cutlets on top. Drizzle a little sauce around the edge and add the oven-baked baby vegetables. Serve at once.

Rosette of Lamb roasted in a Parsley and Truffle Coating

2 whole best end of lamb fillets, trimmed of
  all fat and sinew
salt and freshly ground black pepper
plain flour, for coating
2 eggs, beaten
200 g (7 oz) parsley, finely chopped
1 small bottled black truffle, drained and
  finely chopped
250 g (9 oz) small waxy potatoes
30 g (1 oz) clarified butter
200 ml (7 fl oz) Cabernet Sauvignon
250 g (8 fl oz) well-flavoured jellied lamb
  stock
90 g (3 oz) unsalted butter
250 g (9 oz) baby spinach
40 ml (3 tbsp) virgin olive oil

1 Season the lamb fillets and roll in the flour to coat evenly. Dip into the beaten egg, then roll in the chopped parsley and truffle to coat all over.

2 Add the potatoes (in the skins) to a pan of cold salted water, bring to the boil and cook until tender. Drain, refresh under cold water, then peel away the skins.

3 Meanwhile, heat the clarified butter in a heavy-based pan and seal the lamb on all sides over a low heat.

4 Transfer the lamb to a roasting tin and cook in a preheated oven at 200°C (400°F) mark 6 for 7 minutes. In the meantime, deglaze the pan (in which the lamb was sealed) with the red wine, then add the lamb stock and simmer gently for about 15 minutes until reduced by half.

5 Transfer the lamb to a warmed plate, cover with foil and leave to rest in a warm place for 10 minutes.

6 Meanwhile, melt 30 g (1 oz) of the unsalted butter in a saucepan with a tight-fitting lid, add the baby spinach, stir, then cover and cook until tender.

7 Heat the olive oil in a pan and crush the potatoes into it to mash roughly and warm through.

8 Pass the sauce through a sieve into a clean pan. Heat through, then stir in the remaining butter, a piece at a time.

9 To serve, place a mound of spinach in the centre of each warmed serving plate and spoon the potatoes on top. Slice the lamb and arrange around the potato and spinach. Pour over the sauce and serve at once.

Rack of Lamb with a Coriander and Cream Sauce

2 French-trimmed racks of lamb (each
  with 6-7 bones)
15 ml (1 tbsp) olive oil

Sauce:
15 ml (1 tbsp) olive oil
1 onion, finely chopped
15 coriander seeds
25 g (1 oz) coriander leaves, roughly
  chopped
350 ml (12 fl oz) dry white wine
300 ml (½ pint) homemade lamb stock
100 g (4 oz) full-fat cream cheese
90 ml (3 fl oz) double cream
sea salt and freshly ground black pepper

To Garnish:
coriander sprigs

To Serve:
Potatoes Anna (see page 102)
Asparagus Mousse (see page 90)

1 Heat 15 ml (1 tbsp) olive oil in a large heavy-based frying pan. When it is very hot, add the lamb and quickly seal on all sides.

2 Transfer the lamb to a baking tray and cook in a preheated oven at 220°C (425°F) mark 7 for 8-10 minutes; it should be pink in the centre. Transfer to a warm dish and leave to rest in a warm place for 5-10 minutes before carving.

3 In the meantime, prepare the sauce. Add the oil to the frying pan the lamb was sealed in. When hot, add the onion and cook gently for 5 minutes until softened. Add the coriander seeds and fresh coriander and cook for 1 minute.

4 Deglaze the pan with the white wine, stirring to incorporate any meat juices. Let bubble until reduced by half, then add the lamb stock and, again, reduce by half. Stir in the cream cheese and double cream and reduce until the sauce is thick enough to coat the back of a spoon. Season with salt and pepper to taste. Strain the sauce through a fine sieve.

5 To serve, divide each rack of lamb into cutlets. Spread a pool of sauce on each warmed serving plate and position 3 cutlets on top. Garnish with coriander and serve accompanied by the potatoes anna and asparagus mousse.

Noisettes of Lamb with a Port and Redcurrant Jus

1 lamb loin fillet, about 450-600 g (1-1¼ lb)
30 ml (2 tbsp) olive oil
1 onion, finely chopped
1.2 litres (2 pints) lamb stock
1 rosemary sprig
1 thyme sprig
300 g (10 oz) redcurrants
100 ml (3½ fl oz) port (preferably vintage)
salt and freshly ground black pepper
75 g (3 oz) unsalted butter

To Serve:
redcurrant sprigs, to garnish
Potato and Parsnip Rösti (see page 101)
Green Bean Bundles (see page 91)
Glazed Carrot Ribbons (see page 91)

1 Heat the olive oil in a pan, add the onion and sauté gently until soft but not coloured. Add the lamb stock and herbs and reduce by half.

2 Meanwhile, soak the redcurrants in the port. Add to the stock and reduce again by about half. Pass through a sieve into a clean pan and check the seasoning.

3 Meanwhile, melt 50 g (2 oz) butter in a heavy-based frying pan, add the meat and quickly seal on all sides. Transfer to a roasting tin and cook in a preheated oven at 180°C (350°F) mark 4 for 20 minutes. Let stand in a warm place for 10 minutes.

4 In the meantime, dice the remaining butter. Reheat the sauce and whisk in the diced butter, a piece at a time.

5 To serve, carve the meat into even pieces, allowing three per person. Serve on top of the rösti, surrounded by the sauce. Garnish with redcurrants and serve with the green beans and carrot ribbons.

Fillet of Lamb with a Port and Quince Sauce

15 ml (1 tbsp) oil
4 cloves garlic, peeled and halved
2 whole best end of lamb fillets, trimmed of all fat and sinew
300 ml (½ pint) port
10-15 ml (2-3 tsp) quince jelly, to taste
knob of unsalted butter
salt and freshly ground black pepper

To Serve:
Parsnip and Carrot Cakes (see page 98)
steamed courgette ribbons
Butter-basted Potatoes (see page 101)

1 Heat the oil in a heavy-based frying pan and fry the garlic gently without browning. Then increase the heat, add the lamb fillets and quickly seal and brown all over.

2 Transfer the lamb to a roasting tin and roast in a preheated oven at 200°C (400°F) mark 6 for 12-15 minutes, or longer if you don't like it pink.

3 Meanwhile make the sauce. Return the frying pan to a high heat, add the port and reduce by half. Turn down the heat and add the quince jelly, stirring until it melts into the sauce; keep warm.

4 When the meat is done, remove from the oven, wrap in foil and leave to rest in a warm place for 5 minutes. Add any meat juices from the roasting tin to the sauce. Adjust the seasoning, stir in the butter and strain through a muslin-lined sieve.

5 Carve the meat into slices, allowing 4-5 per person. Place a parsnip and carrot cake on each warmed serving plate and arrange the meat on top. Add some courgette ribbons and surround with the sauce. Serve with the potatoes.

Roast Noisette of Lamb with a Cranberry and Port Sauce, Cranberry and Orange Salsa and Peppered Pecans

Make sure the butcher gives you the bones which are needed for the stock.

2 whole best end of lamb fillets, each about 200 g (7 oz)
salt and freshly ground black pepper
knob of unsalted butter
15 ml (1 tbsp) olive oil

Cranberry and Port Sauce:
50 g (2 oz) butter
50 g (2 oz) shallots, finely chopped
125 g (4 oz) button mushrooms, sliced
125 g (4 oz) cranberries
300 ml (½ pint) port
300 ml (½ pint) lamb stock (see below)
30 ml (2 tbsp) cranberry jelly with port
60 ml (2 fl oz) orange juice
few drops of sherry vinegar (optional)
25 g (1 oz) butter, chilled and cubed

Cranberry and Orange Salsa:
175 g (6 oz) cranberries (fresh or frozen and thawed)
120 ml (4 fl oz) orange juice (approximately)
50-75 g (2-3 oz) sugar, to taste
finely grated zest and juice of 1 lime
60 ml (4 tbsp) chopped coriander
½-1 red chilli, deseeded and finely chopped
1 orange, peeled and segmented (all white pith removed)

Peppered Pecans:
50 g (2 oz) shelled pecan nuts
15 ml (1 tbsp) unsalted butter, melted
sprinkling of crushed dried pepper flakes
5 ml (1 tsp) salt

To Serve:
Spiced Sweet Potato Purée (see page 97)
Glazed Stir-fried Vegetables (see page 78)

1 To make the sauce, heat the butter in a pan, add the shallots and sweat until soft. Add the mushrooms and cranberries and cook gently for about 5 minutes. Add the port, bring to the boil and reduce by half. Add the stock, skim if necessary and cook for 30 minutes, reducing the sauce down by about one third. Pass the sauce through a sieve and return to a clean pan. Add the cranberry jelly, orange juice and a few drops of sherry vinegar if necessary to sharpen the taste.

2 To make the salsa, put the cranberries into a saucepan and add just enough orange juice to cover. Bring to a simmer and cook until the berries start to burst. Immediately remove from the heat and add the sugar to taste. Drain off the orange juice. Turn the cranberries into a serving bowl and stir in the lime zest and juice, chopped coriander and chilli. Chop the orange segments and stir into the salsa. Set aside to allow the flavours to develop.

3 To prepare the pecans, toss with the melted butter, chilli flakes and salt, then spread out on a baking tray. Bake in a preheated oven at 180°C (350°F) mark 4 for 8-10 minutes, until lightly browned – watch carefully as they quickly burn! Drain off excess butter and allow the pecan nuts to cool slightly.

4 To cook the lamb, season generously with salt and pepper. Melt a knob of butter and 15 ml (1 tbsp) olive oil in a heavy-based frying pan, add the lamb and sear until browned on all sides. Transfer to a roasting tin and cook in a preheated oven at 220°C (425°F) mark 7 for no longer than 10 minutes. Wrap the lamb in foil and leave to rest in a warm place for 10 minutes.

5 Just before serving, reheat the sauce and whisk in the chilled butter, a piece at a time. Check the seasoning.

6 Slice the lamb into medallions and arrange on warmed serving plates, allowing 4 or 5 slices per serving. Pour the sauce over the meat and garnish with the pecan nuts. Serve with the cranberry and orange salsa, sweet potato purée and glazed stir-fried vegetables.

Lamb Stock: Put the lamb bones and 225 g (8 oz) scrag end or lamb trimmings into a large roasting tin and cook in a preheated oven at 220°C (425°F) mark 7 until beginning to colour. Add 2 large onions, chopped; 3 large carrots, chopped; 3 sticks celery, chopped; cook for a further 15 minutes. Pour off all the fat from the tin. Transfer the mixture to a large saucepan, deglaze the roasting tin with 120 ml (4 fl oz) dry white wine, then add to the saucepan. Add enough cold water to cover, bring to the boil and skim. Add 4 peeled, deseeded and diced tomatoes; 4 peeled cloves garlic, a bouquet garni and a few crushed black peppercorns. Simmer for 1½ hours, skimming from time to time. Strain the stock through a fine sieve, let cool and chill. Remove the fat from the surface and use as required.

Fillet of Lamb coated in Pesto and wrapped in Parma Ham

2 best end of lamb fillets, trimmed
30 ml (2 tbsp) olive oil
8-10 slices of Parma ham (evenly sized)

Pesto:
120 ml (4 fl oz) olive oil
50 g (2 oz) pine nuts
40 g (1½ oz) Parmesan cheese, freshly grated
1 clove garlic, peeled
1 good bunch of basil, leaves only

Sauce:
4 large ripe tomatoes, chopped
60 ml (2 fl oz) white wine
60 ml (2 fl oz) red wine
60 ml (2 fl oz) lamb stock
30-45 (2-3 tbsp) double cream
5 ml (1 tsp) tomato purée
salt and freshly ground black pepper
25-30 g (1-2 oz) butter, chilled and diced

Parsnip Crisps:
2-3 parsnips, peeled
oil for deep-frying

To Serve:
Roasted Vegetable Salad (see page 88)
Sweet Potato Purée (see page 100)

1 Heat the 30 ml (2 tbsp) oil in a heavy-based frying pan. Add the lamb fillets and quickly seal on all sides over a high heat; remove and set aside.

2 To make the pesto, heat 30 ml (2 tbsp) of the olive oil in the frying pan, add the pine nuts and fry until golden; remove with a slotted spoon. Allow to cool, then put into a blender or food processor with the Parmesan, garlic, basil and remaining oil. Process to the desired consistency.

3 Spread the pesto over the lamb fillets to coat evenly, then wrap in the slices of Parma ham to enclose. Secure with wooden cocktail sticks if necessary. Cook in a preheated oven at 220°C (425°F) mark 7 for approximately 20 minutes for pink lamb (or less if you like it rare).

4 Meanwhile, make the sauce. Put the tomatoes in a pan with the white wine, red wine and lamb stock. Bring to a simmer and cook gently for about 20 minutes, mashing the tomatoes down to a pulp. Pass through a sieve and return to the pan. Add the cream, tomato purée and seasoning to taste. If the sauce is too thick, thin with a little white wine.

5 Once the lamb is cooked, cover lightly with foil and leave to rest in a warm place for 5-10 minutes. Just before serving, prepare the parsnip crisps. Finely slice the parsnips; heat the oil for deep-frying. When it is very hot, deep-fry the parsnip slices in batches until crisp. Drain on kitchen paper and sprinkle with salt to taste. Keep hot while cooking the remainder.

6 To serve, carve the lamb into 1 cm (½ inch) thick slices and arrange on warmed serving plates. Pour on the sauce and garnish with the parsnip crisps. Serve with the roasted vegetable salad and sweet potato purée.

Mediterranean Vegetables stuffed with Meat and Rice, cooked in a Lemon and Mint Broth

Stuffing:
225 g (8 oz) minced beef or lamb
125 g (4 oz) short-grain pudding rice, washed
5 ml (1 tsp) dried mint
2.5 ml (½ tsp) salt
25 g (1 oz) pine nuts, lightly toasted

Vegetables:
4 courgettes, trimmed
2 small aubergines, trimmed
2 red peppers
20 vine leaves, blanched

Broth:
few lean lamb bones
1.2 litres (2 pints) well-flavoured vegetable stock
juice and grated zest of 3 lemons
15 ml (1 tbsp) dried mint
5 ml (1 tsp) salt

To Serve:
Greek-style yogurt
Okra in Tomato Sauce (see page 93)

1 Mix all the ingredients for the stuffing together in a large bowl.

2 Halve the courgettes and aubergines lengthwise and carefully scoop out the centres, ensuring that the base of each half is not pierced. Halve the peppers crosswise and remove the cores and seeds. Trim off a sliver from the base of each pepper cup to ensure it stands upright. Separate the vine leaves and trim off any thick stalks.

3 Lay the lamb bones in the bottom of a large, heavy-based pan and cover with four of the vine leaves, laying them flat to make a platform for the stuffed vegetables.

4 First, stuff the rest of the vine leaves. Place a teaspoonful of the mixture at the base of the leaf. Fold the sides of the leaf over the filling and roll up very tightly, like a cigar. Lay it in the centre of the pan, seam-side down. Repeat with the remaining vine leaves, arranging the rolls in a circular pattern around the base of the pan.

5 Fill the peppers, courgettes and aubergines with the remaining stuffing and arrange upside-down on top of the flat vine leaves. Pack them in very tightly as this helps keep the stuffing in place and retains the shape of the vegetables; if there are not enough vegetables to fill the diameter of the pan, fill the gaps with potatoes.

6 In a separate pan, heat the stock with the lemon zest and juice, mint and salt. Pour this carefully over the vegetables and cover with a plate and a weight. Put on the lid and simmer for 30 minutes.

7 To serve, remove the lid, weight and plate. Carefully pour off any excess stock and reserve. Invert a large deep serving dish over the pan. Using oven gloves, turn the pan and plate over, then lift off the pan to turn out the vegetables onto the dish. Remove the lamb bones and flat vine leaves. Pour the extra stock back over the vegetables. Serve accompanied by a bowl of yogurt, and the okra in tomato sauce.

Baked Kibbeh
*(Lamb, Bulghar Wheat, Onion
and Pine Nut Cake)*

If possible, ask your butcher to put the
lamb through the mincer twice to ensure a
fine texture.

Filling:
125 g (4 oz) lean finely minced lamb
50 g (2 oz) pine nuts
1 small onion, finely chopped
2.5 ml (½ tsp) ground cinnamon
2.5 ml (½ tsp) mixed spice
2.5 ml (½ tsp) salt
freshly ground black pepper

'Cake':
350 g (12 oz) lean finely minced lamb
175 g (6 oz) bulghar wheat, rinsed
1 large onion, grated
*1 large red pepper, cored, deseeded and
   grated*
5 ml (1 tsp) ground cinnamon
5 ml (1 tsp) mixed spice
2.5 ml (½ tsp) salt
30 ml (2 tbsp) extra-virgin olive oil

To Serve:
Lebanese-style Ratatouille (see page 92)

1 First make the filling. Dry-fry the pine
nuts in a large heavy-based frying pan over
a low heat until lightly toasted; watch
carefully as they burn easily. Tip the nuts
out onto a plate.

2 Add the minced lamb to the pan and fry
without oil, stirring, until browned. Add
the onion and spices and cook gently for
5 minutes. Season with salt and pepper and
add the pine nuts to the mixture. Stir well
and set aside.

3 Put all the 'cake' ingredients, except the
olive oil, in a large bowl. Mix thoroughly,
squeezing the mixture with your hands
until the ingredients are well combined and
form a paste.

4 Brush an 18-20 cm (7-8 inch) cake tin
with olive oil. Dip your hands into iced
water, then spread half of the paste in the
cake tin with your hands, ensuring any
joins are well sealed. Spoon the filling
mixture evenly on top, cover with the
remaining paste, smoothing the surface
with wet hands.

5 With a sharp knife, score a deep,
diamond pattern on the surface of the cake
and drizzle the olive oil over the top. Run a
knife around the edge of the tin; this helps
to stop the mixture sticking. Bake in a
preheated oven at 200°C (400°F) mark 6
for 1 hour.

6 Serve hot or cold, cut into slices,
accompanied by the ratatouille.

Note: The kibbeh can be prepared ahead
to the end of stage 4, refrigerated and
cooked later in the day. In this case the
filling must be completely cooled before
the dish is assembled.

Marinated Pork on Puy Lentils with a Truffle Sauce

450-600 g (1-1¼ lb) pork tenderloin

Marinade:
15 ml (1 tbsp) soy sauce
15 ml (1 tbsp) sherry
5 ml (1 tsp) red bean curd
5 ml (1 tsp) thin honey

For the Lentils:
100 g (3½ oz) Puy lentils, rinsed in cold water
1 clove garlic, crushed
15 ml (1 tbsp) olive oil

Sauce:
200 g (7 oz) butter, chilled and diced
1 shallot, finely chopped
100 ml (3½ fl oz) dry sherry
10 ml (2 tsp) truffle paste
salt and freshly ground black pepper

Deep-fried Leeks:
1 leek, trimmed
sunflower oil, for deep-frying
flour, for dusting

To Serve:
Courgette Ribbons (see page 91)

1 Lay the pork tenderloin in a shallow dish. For the marinade, mix together the soy sauce, sherry, red bean curd and honey and drizzle evenly over the meat. Cover and leave to marinate in a cool place for at least 3 hours, turning occasionally.

2 Place the pork on a trivet over a roasting tin and cook in a preheated oven at 200°C (400°F) mark 6 for 45 minutes.

3 In the meantime, put the lentils in a saucepan with 350 ml (12 fl oz) water. Bring to the boil and boil for 10 minutes, then lower the heat and simmer for 30-35 minutes until just tender.

4 Meanwhile, make the sauce. Melt a small knob of butter in another pan, add the shallot and sweat gently until softened, then add the dry sherry; turn up the heat and reduce to a syrup. Add 5 ml (1 tsp) cold water, then whisk in half of the butter a piece at a time. Add the truffle paste, then gradually whisk in the remainder of the butter; check the seasoning. Keep the sauce warm or it will 'split'.

5 Meanwhile, cut the leek into 5 cm (2 inch) lengths and finely slice lengthwise. Heat the sunflower oil in a deep pan. Dust the leek with seasoned flour and deep-fry in the hot oil for 10 seconds or until crisp. Remove and drain on kitchen paper; keep hot until ready to serve.

6 When the lentils are cooked, drain off any excess water and place in a saucepan with the garlic and olive oil; heat gently.

7 To serve, finely slice the pork. Spoon the lentils onto warmed serving plates, arrange the pork on top and surround with the sauce. Garnish with deep-fried leek and serve immediately, with courgette ribbons.

Tenderloin of Pork with a Juniper and Thyme Crust

For the pork noodles, ask your butcher for a piece of pork rind, 20 cm (8 inches) square; it doesn't matter if it is in more than one piece. Leave it to dry overnight.

2 pork tenderloins, trimmed of any fat and sinew
piece of pork rind, fat removed (see above)
1 small skinless chicken breast fillet, roughly chopped
1 egg white
150 ml (¼ pint) double cream (approximately)
10 juniper berries, crushed
few thyme sprigs
60 g (2½ oz) soft white breadcrumbs
salt and freshly ground black pepper

Madeira Sauce:
500 ml (16 fl oz) Madeira
500 ml (16 fl oz) chicken stock (see below)
knob of butter

To Serve:
steamed baby spinach

1 Wrap the pork tenderloins individually in cling film and refrigerate for 1 hour; this helps them to retain a good shape.

2 Meanwhile, make the sauce. Bring the Madeira to the boil in a saucepan and reduce by half. Add the chicken stock and reduce again by one third. Season with salt and pepper to taste. Whisk in a knob of butter and set aside; keep warm.

3 Put the chicken breast and egg white in a food processor and process until smooth. Add the cream, a little at a time, processing until you have a smooth firm paste; it may not be necessary to add all of the cream.

4 Finely chop the juniper berries with the thyme leaves. Mix with the breadcrumbs and seasoning.

5 Unwrap the pork and spread all over with the chicken mousseline, then roll in the herb and breadcrumb mixture to coat thoroughly; refrigerate until ready to cook.

6 To prepare the crispy pork 'noodles', cut the rind into very thin strips, as long as the piece of rind will allow, using kitchen scissors. Sprinkle with salt and place in a shallow baking tin. Cook in a preheated oven at 220°C (425°F) mark 7 for about 15 minutes until the noodles are crispy and curly; keep hot. Reduce the oven setting to 180°C (350°F) mark 4.

7 Lay the pork tenderloins in a roasting tin and cook in the preheated oven for about 30 minutes. Transfer the pork to a warmed plate, cover lightly with foil and leave to rest in a warm place for 10 minutes. Reheat the sauce if necessary.

8 To serve, carve the pork into 2 cm (¾ inch) thick slices. Serve on a bed of baby spinach, topped with the crispy 'noodles'. Spoon the Madeira sauce around the pork and serve at once.

Chicken Stock: Put 2 kg (4½ lb) chicken bones in a roasting tin and roast in a hot oven until golden brown. Dice 1 large onion, 2 leeks, 2 carrots, 2 celery sticks, 6 tomatoes and 2 cloves garlic, add to the roasting tin and cook on a medium heat for 15 minutes. Transfer to a large saucepan, add 500 ml (16 fl oz) dry white wine and reduce by half. Add 3 litres (5 pints) water and a bouquet garni. Bring to the boil and simmer for 4 hours, skimming frequently. Strain through a muslin-lined sieve into a clean pan. Reduce to 500 ml (16 fl oz). Leave to cool, then refrigerate.

Roast Pork with Sage and a Raspberry and Redcurrant Sauce

2 pork tenderloins (cut from the thick end),
  each about 300 g (10 oz)
25 g (1 oz) butter
3 shallots, finely chopped
15 ml (1 tbsp) fresh breadcrumbs
15 red pepper berries, crushed
30 ml (2 tbsp) finely chopped sage
salt and freshly ground black pepper
pinch of freshly grated nutmeg
8 rashers streaky bacon, derinded
150 ml (¼ pint) port
15 ml (1 tbsp) redcurrant jelly
30 ml (2 tbsp) redcurrants
60 ml (4 tbsp) raspberries

To Serve:
Oven-rösti Potatoes (see page 104)
carrots and courgettes

1 Slice each pork tenderloin lengthwise about halfway through and open out flat. Heat half of the butter in a pan, add two thirds of the shallots and cook gently until softened. Remove from the heat and stir in the breadcrumbs, red pepper berries, sage, salt, pepper and nutmeg. Spread this stuffing evenly over one fillet and place the other one on top.

2 Stretch the bacon rasher with the back of a knife, then wrap around the pork. Place in a roasting tin and cook in a preheated oven at 190°C (375°F) mark 5 for 50 minutes.

3 Meanwhile, make the sauce. Heat the remaining butter in a pan, add the rest of the shallot and cook until softened. Add the port and reduce slightly. Add the redcurrant jelly, redcurrants and raspberries and simmer until the fruit is soft. Pass the sauce through a fine sieve into a pan; keep warm.

4 Once the pork is cooked, cover with foil and leave to rest in a warm place for 10 minutes. To serve, carve the pork into slices and arrange on warmed serving plates. Pour the sauce around the meat and serve with the vegetables.

Roast Tenderloin of Pork with a Prune and Wine Sauce

2 pork tenderloins, each about 350 g (12 oz)
8 Agen prunes, stoned and quartered
150 ml (¼ pint) earl grey tea (made with
    2 teabags)
50 g (2 oz) unsalted butter
2 shallots, chopped
2 cloves garlic, crushed
1 bay leaf
1 thyme sprig
salt and freshly ground black pepper
25 ml (5 tsp) cognac
150 ml (¼ pint) red wine
5-6 spare rib bones, roasted
400 ml (14 fl oz) chicken stock
200 ml (7 fl oz) water

To Serve:
Olive Oil Mashed Potato (see page 103)
stir-fried cabbage
parsnip chips

1 Soak the prunes in the earl grey tea for at least 1 hour.

2 To make the sauce, preheat a large heavy-based frying pan. When hot, add half of the butter and heat until foaming. Add the chopped shallots, garlic, bay leaf, thyme and pepper and cook until well browned. Pour in the cognac and cook until all the liquid has evaporated. Add the wine and pork bones. Cook on a medium heat, again until the liquid is completely evaporated. Add the stock and water, bring to the boil and simmer for approximately 50 minutes until the sauce is well reduced and thickened. Skim off any fat and pass the sauce through a sieve into a small pan. Drain the prunes and add to the sauce; keep warm.

3 To cook the pork, heat the remaining butter in a heavy-based ovenproof frying pan or roasting tin on a medium heat until foaming. Add the pork tenderloins and sear, turning to brown on all sides.

4 Transfer to a preheated oven at 180°C (350°F) mark 4 and roast for approximately 20 minutes until the pork is cooked thoroughly. Cover and leave to rest in a warm place for 5-10 minutes.

5 Reheat the sauce. Carve the pork into thick slices and arrange on warmed serving plates. Pour on the prune and wine sauce and serve with the mashed potato, stir-fried cabbage and parsnip chips.

Note: The inclusion of pork bones in the sauce isn't essential but it does improve the flavour. Before adding, roast them in a preheated hot oven at 230°C (450°F) mark 8 for about 20 minutes.

Accompaniments

Salsa Stacks

Mini Tortillas:
50 g (2 oz) cornmeal
40 g (1½ oz) plain flour
5 ml (1 tsp) salt
1 clove garlic, crushed
15 ml (1 tbsp) olive oil
15-30 ml (1-2 tbsp) milk
freshly ground black pepper

Salsa:
½ red onion, peeled
2 ripe tomatoes, skinned
1 ripe avocado, peeled, halved and stoned
2.5 cm (1 inch) piece cucumber
30 ml (2 tbsp) coriander leaves
juice of ½ lime

1 To make the tortillas, sift the cornmeal and flour into a bowl. Add the salt and garlic. Stir in the olive oil, milk and pepper to form a firm dough.

2 Lightly knead the tortilla dough on a floured board. Roll out very thinly and stamp out 12 circles, using a 4 cm (1½ inch) cutter.

3 Preheat the grill to its highest setting. Place the mini tortillas on a small baking sheet and grill for about 30 seconds on each side. Transfer to a wire rack to cool.

4 To make the salsa, finely and evenly chop the onion, tomatoes, avocado, cucumber and coriander; mix together in a bowl. Sprinkle with the lime juice and season with salt and pepper to taste.

5 To serve, sandwich the tortillas together in stacks of three with the salsa.

Roasted Vegetable Salad

1 aubergine
1 courgette
olive oil, for cooking
2 red peppers
1 clove garlic, finely chopped
few rosemary sprigs

Dressing:
15 ml (1 tbsp) balsamic vinegar
20 ml (4 tsp) olive oil
salt and freshly ground black pepper

1 Peel the aubergine and cut crosswise into 5 mm (¼ inch) thick slices. Cut the courgette into 3 mm (⅛ inch) slices. Heat a little olive oil in a heavy-based frying pan and fry the aubergine slices, in batches if necessary, until golden brown on both sides; remove and set aside. Repeat with the courgette slices.

2 Meanwhile, roast the red peppers in a preheated oven at 180°C (350°F) mark 4 for about 30 minutes until beginning to lose their shape. When cooked, pierce each pepper to release the juices into a bowl; set aside. Halve, core and deseed the peppers, then cut into strips.

3 Arrange the peppers, aubergine and courgette slices in an ovenproof dish. Brush with a little more olive oil and scatter the chopped garlic and rosemary over them. Bake in the oven for 40 minutes.

4 Meanwhile, put the ingredients for the dressing in a screw-topped jar with the reserved pepper juices and shake vigorously to combine.

5 Drizzle the dressing over the vegetables and serve hot, warm or cold.

Glazed Stir-fried Vegetables with Herb Butter

8 baby carrots
8 baby corn cobs
12 French beans, trimmed
50 g (2 oz) frozen peas, thawed
12 asparagus tips
2 small or 1 large courgette, cut into batons
½ red pepper, deseeded and cut into fine strips

Herb Butter:
50 g (2 oz) unsalted butter
grated zest of ½ lemon
7.5 ml (1½ tsp) lemon juice
22 ml (1½ tbsp) chopped flat-leaf parsley
few snipped chives

1 First make the herb butter. Put all the ingredients into a food processor and whizz to amalgamate. Put the herb butter onto a piece of greaseproof paper and roll into a cracker shape. Chill until firm.

2 Briefly blanch the carrots, corn cobs, French beans and peas separately in boiling salted water until *al dente* – cooked but still firm to the bite. Refresh under cold water; drain thoroughly. (The asparagus and courgettes require minimal blanching.)

3 Preheat a wok. Add all the vegetables with a few slices of herb butter (see note). Toss until warmed through and glazed. Serve at once.

Note: You will only need to use about half of the butter; keep the rest wrapped in the refrigerator for another occasion.

Oven-baked Baby Vegetables

selection of baby vegetables (onions, courgettes, turnips, carrots etc – see note)
60 ml (2 fl oz) olive oil
2 rosemary sprigs, chopped
1 thyme sprig, chopped
1 clove garlic, thinly sliced
squeeze of lemon juice
salt and freshly ground black pepper

1 Prepare the vegetables as necessary, peeling the onions only. Cut any larger vegetables, such as small turnips, into manageable pieces.

2 Put the vegetables into a bowl and add the oil, herbs, garlic, lemon juice and seasoning. Mix thoroughly, to ensure all of the vegetables are coated with oil.

3 Transfer to a shallow baking tin and bake in a preheated oven at 200°C (400°F) mark 6 for approximately 40 minutes or until tender and nicely browned.

Note: Allow 1 or 2 of each vegetable per person.

Asparagus Mousse

350 g (12 oz) asparagus, trimmed
sea salt and freshly ground black pepper
25 g (1 oz) butter
1 onion, finely diced
2.5 cm (1 inch) piece fresh root ginger,
*   peeled and finely chopped*
25 g (1 oz) lean lamb fillet (small offcut),
*   finely chopped*
1 egg
25 ml (1 fl oz) double cream
15 ml (1 tbsp) olive oil

To Garnish:
12 asparagus tips

1 Cut the asparagus into 5 cm (2 inch) lengths and cook in boiling salted water for 10 minutes or until tender. Drain thoroughly and purée in a food processor or blender. Transfer to a fine-meshed sieve to drain off any excess liquid.

2 Melt half of the butter in a pan, add the onion and ginger and sweat gently until softened; leave to cool. Return the asparagus to the food processor or blender and add the cooled onion and ginger mixture, the lamb, egg, cream and plenty of seasoning. Process thoroughly until smooth.

3 Divide the mixture between 4 dariole moulds (see note), leaving a 5 mm (¼ inch) margin at the top. Tap each dariole firmly on the work surface to exclude any air pockets.

4 Stand the dariole moulds in a wide shallow saucepan (or deep frying pan) and pour in sufficient boiling water to come two-thirds up the sides of the moulds. Bring to a simmer and cover the pan loosely with foil. Simmer for 30-40 minutes or until a sharp knife inserted into the centre comes out cleanly.

5 Shortly before serving, prepare the garnish. Pan-fry the asparagus tips in the remaining 15 g (½ oz) butter and 15 ml (1 tbsp) olive oil until tender and lightly browned.

6 To serve, run a knife around the edge of each mousse and turn out onto warmed serving plates. Garnish with the sautéed asparagus tips.

Note: If you haven't any dariole moulds, use greased small 120 ml (4 fl oz) capacity ramekins instead.

Lemon and Mustard-dressed Leaves

50 g (2 oz) baby lamb's lettuce

Dressing:
30 ml (2 tbsp) olive oil
15 ml (1 tbsp) lemon juice
5 ml (1 tsp) Dijon mustard
salt and cracked black pepper

1 Whisk together all the ingredients for the dressing.

2 Toss the leaves in half of the dressing, reserving the remainder for drizzling around the main dish.

Courgette Ribbons

2 courgettes
olive oil, for marinating
freshly ground black pepper

1 Using a swivel vegetable peeler, pare the courgettes into long thin ribbons. Place in a shallow dish and add sufficient olive oil to cover. Season with pepper. Leave to marinate for 20 minutes.

2 Using a slotted spoon, transfer the courgettes to a clean baking dish and roast in a preheated oven at 190°C (375°F) mark 5 for approximately 16 minutes until crisp and golden.

Green Bean Bundles

1 leek
300 g (10 oz) French beans
salt and freshly ground black pepper

1 Remove and discard the 2 outer layers from the leek. Blanch the leek in boiling water for 1 minute, then refresh in cold water. Drain thoroughly and cut into 1 cm (½ inch) strips.

2 Trim the beans to an even length. Add to a pan of boiling salted water and simmer for 4-5 minutes until just tender.

3 Drain the beans, divide into bundles and tie a 'leek ribbon' around each bundle. Serve at once.

Spaghetti of Carrot and Courgette

225 g (8 oz) carrots, peeled
225 g (8 oz) courgettes, halved and deseeded
25 g (1 oz) unsalted butter
salt and freshly ground black pepper

1 Slice the carrots and courgettes into thin 'spaghetti' using a mandoline or sharp knife.

2 Cook the carrots in boiling salted water for 4 minutes, add the courgettes and boil for a further 2 minutes. Drain and refresh in iced water. Drain thoroughly.

3 When ready to serve, place the blanched vegetables in a pan with the butter. Cover and shake over a moderate heat, until thoroughly reheated. Season with salt and pepper to taste. Serve immediately.

Glazed Carrot Ribbons

25 g (1 oz) unsalted butter
30 ml (2 tbsp) chopped parsley
175 g (6 oz) carrots, peeled
salt and freshly ground black pepper

1 Melt the butter, allow to cool, then skim off any froth from the surface and add the parsley.

2 Using a swivel potato peeler, pare the carrots into long, thin ribbons. Add to a pan of boiling salted water and simmer for 2-3 minutes until just tender.

3 Drain thoroughly and toss with the parsley butter and salt and pepper to taste. Serve at once.

Lebanese-style Ratatouille with Seared Vegetables

1 aubergine, trimmed
2 courgettes, trimmed
1 red pepper, halved, cored and seeded
60 ml (4 tbsp) extra-virgin olive oil
4 cloves garlic, crushed
salt and freshly ground black pepper
250 ml (8 fl oz) well-flavoured vegetable
    stock
10 ml (2 tsp) tomato paste
4 large tomatoes, skinned and chopped
1 onion, finely chopped
1 small bunch mint sprigs, chopped
5 ml (1 tsp) dried mint
squeeze of lemon juice

To Garnish:
15 ml (1 tbsp) chopped mint

1 Using a sharp knife and slicing on the diagonal, cut 4 slices from the aubergine and 8 slices from the courgettes. Cut 4 large diamonds from the peppers. Reserve the vegetable trimmings.

2 Lay these vegetable slices in a shallow dish, add the olive oil, garlic, salt and pepper and leave to marinate for about 30 minutes.

3 Meanwhile, finely chop the vegetable trimmings. Pour the stock into a saucepan and add the tomato paste, tomatoes, onion and vegetable trimmings. Add the fresh and dried mint, bring to the boil and simmer for 20 minutes until fairly thick. Check the seasoning.

4 Preheat a griddle pan and brush with oil. Remove the sliced vegetables from the marinade and cook them on the griddle in batches if necessary for 5 minutes until caramelised and charred on both sides.

5 Arrange the griddled vegetable slices to one side of each serving plate and spoon the sauce around them. Finish off with a squeeze of lemon juice and a sprinkling of chopped mint.

Okra in a Tomato Sauce

450 g (1 lb) okra
45 ml (3 tbsp) olive oil
1 large onion, chopped
1 clove garlic, crushed
2.5 ml (½ tsp) ground cinnamon
4 large tomatoes, skinned and chopped
15 ml (1 tbsp) tomato paste
2.5 ml (½ tsp) salt
15 ml (1 tbsp) chopped parsley

1 Carefully trim the stalks and tips from the okra, being careful to avoid cutting off too much – or you will release the gelatinous juices in the pods.

2 Heat the oil in a large frying pan, add the okra and fry for a few minutes until they turn bright green; remove and keep warm.

3 Add the onion, garlic and cinnamon to the pan and fry for 2 minutes, then return the okra to the pan and add the tomatoes, tomato paste and salt.

4 Cover and simmer gently for about 20 minutes. The sauce will become very thick, so stir carefully from time to time to prevent the okra from sticking. A little boiling water can be added if the sauce is too thick. Ideally, the okra should be coated with tomato, without any thin sauce left in the pan.

5 Serve at room temperature, or warm if preferred, sprinkled with chopped parsley.

Fennel, Tomato and Chervil Casserole

350 g (12 oz) fennel, trimmed
30 ml (2 tbsp) olive oil
4 plum tomatoes
few drops of lemon juice (optional)
salt and freshly ground black pepper
45 ml (3 tbsp) finely chopped chervil

1 Cut the fennel lengthwise into 5 mm (¼ inch) slices. Heat the olive oil in a small flameproof casserole or heavy-based pan, add the fennel, cover and stew gently over a low heat for 20 minutes.

2 Purée the tomatoes in a food processor or blender, then pass through a sieve into a bowl to remove the seeds; taste for acidity and, if necessary, sharpen the puréed tomatoes with a few drops of lemon juice. Season with salt and pepper to taste.

3 Just before serving, stir the puréed tomato and chervil into the fennel and heat through. Check the seasoning.

Caramelised Fennel

2 fennel bulbs, trimmed
50 g (2 oz) butter
10 ml (2 tsp) olive oil
5 ml (1 tsp) demerara sugar, or to taste
60 ml (4 tbsp) apple juice
10 ml (2 tsp) cider vinegar
salt and freshly ground black pepper

1 Slice the fennel and steam (preferably in a fan steamer) over a pan of boiling water for approximately 10 minutes until almost tender.

2 Melt the butter and oil in a clean pan, add the sugar and fennel slices, stir and sauté for about 5 minutes until golden.

3 Add the apple juice and cider vinegar and simmer, uncovered, for 5 minutes or until the cooking juices caramelise and turn golden. Season with salt and pepper to taste. Serve at once.

Deep-fried Leeks

2 medium leeks, trimmed
plain flour, for coating
salt and freshly ground black pepper
groundnut oil, for frying

1 Shred the leeks finely into julienne strips. Put some seasoned flour into a bag, add the leeks and shake to coat evenly.

2 Heat a 4 cm (1½ inch) depth of oil in a small heavy-based saucepan until a light haze appears. Add the leeks and deep-fry for 2-3 minutes until golden and crisp. Drain well on kitchen paper. Season with salt and pepper and serve at once.

Butter Beans and Leeks in Noilly Prat

75 g (3 oz) butter beans, soaked overnight in cold water
50 g (2 oz) butter (approximately)
1 large leek, finely sliced
salt and freshly ground black pepper
½ glass Noilly Prat
75 ml (5 tbsp) double cream
30-60 ml (2-4 tbsp) milk

1 Drain the butter beans, rinse thoroughly and place in a saucepan. Cover with plenty of fresh cold water, bring to the boil and boil steadily for 10 minutes. Lower the heat, cover and simmer for a further 40 minutes or until the butter beans are cooked through.

2 Melt the butter in another pan, add the sliced leek and sauté gently until softened.

3 Add the cooked beans to the leek and fry gently for a few minutes, adding a little more butter if required. Season with salt and pepper to taste.

4 Stir in the Noilly Prat and cream and cook gently for about 10 minutes, adding enough milk to give a creamy consistency.

Red Cabbage with Juniper

30 ml (2 tbsp) olive oil
1 onion, finely chopped
6 juniper berries, lightly crushed
½ large red cabbage, cored and finely
    shredded
150 ml (¼ pint) vegetable stock
15 ml (1 tbsp) redcurrant jelly
15 ml (1 tbsp) white wine vinegar
salt and freshly ground black pepper
1 eating apple, peeled, cored and finely
    chopped

1 Heat the oil in a medium heavy-based
pan. Add the onion and fry gently until
softened but not brown. Add the juniper
berries, stir and fry until they begin to
release their aroma.

2 Add the red cabbage, stock, redcurrant
jelly, vinegar, salt and pepper. Bring to the
boil, cover and simmer for 15-20 minutes.

3 Add the finely chopped apple, re-cover
and cook for a further 10 minutes. Check
the seasoning before serving.

Buttered Savoy Cabbage

1 Savoy cabbage, cored and finely shredded
salt and freshly ground black pepper
25 g (1 oz) butter
15 ml (1 tbsp) mild grainy mustard

1 Cook the cabbage in boiling salted water
until just tender; drain thoroughly.

2 Heat the butter and mustard together in
a pan, add the cabbage and toss gently.
Check the seasoning and serve.

Buttered Cabbage

450 g (1 lb) Savoy or other green cabbage,
    cored and shredded
55 g (2 oz) unsalted butter
salt and freshly ground white pepper

1 Add the cabbage to a pan of lightly
salted boiling water and par-boil for about
2 minutes. Drain and refresh in cold water,
then squeeze dry.

2 Melt the butter in a pan, add the
cabbage and sauté for about 2 minutes.
Season with salt and pepper to taste. Serve
at once.

Gratin of Celeriac and Parsnip

½ celeriac, peeled
3 parsnips, peeled, halved and cored
salt and freshly ground black pepper
freshly grated nutmeg
400 ml (14 fl oz) single cream

1 Finely slice the celeriac and parsnips.
Season with salt, pepper and nutmeg.

2 Arrange the celeriac and parsnip slices
in alternate layers in 4 ramekins. Top up
with the single cream.

3 Cover with foil and bake in a preheated
oven at 180°C (350°F) mark 4 for about
45 minutes, until tender. Unmould onto
warmed plates to serve.

Glazed Onions

200 g (7 oz) baby onions (unpeeled)
15 g (½ oz) unsalted butter
5 ml (1 tsp) sugar
salt and freshly ground black pepper

1 Blanch the onions in boiling water for 1 minute, then drain and peel off the skins.

2 Combine the onions, butter and sugar in a small sauté pan over a low heat. Season with salt and pepper. Cover and cook for 15-20 minutes, until the onions are tender.

Stir-fried Red Onions with Cabbage and Bacon

45 ml (3 tbsp) olive oil
1 large red onion, finely sliced
225 g (8 oz) streaky bacon, derinded
350 g (12 oz) Savoy cabbage leaves, cored and finely shredded
salt and freshly ground black pepper

1 Heat the oil in a large pan. Add the onion and fry gently until softened.

2 Meanwhile, cut the bacon into thin strips and grill until lightly browned.

3 Add the bacon and cabbage to the onion and stir-fry for about 5 minutes until the cabbage is cooked, but still firm to the bite. Season with salt and pepper to taste. Serve immediately.

Note: For convenience, the recipe can be prepared in advance to the end of stage 2, then finished just before serving.

Julienne of Red Onion and Red Pepper

3 red onions, thinly sliced
15 g (½ oz) unsalted butter
350 ml (12 fl oz) white wine
2 large red peppers, halved, cored and deseeded

1 Sauté the onions in the butter for 2-3 minutes. Turn the heat down as low as possible and add 30 ml (2 tbsp) of the wine. Continue to simmer for 1½ hours adding the wine in small amounts throughout the cooking to prevent the onions from drying out. When cooked, the onions should be transparent.

2 Meanwhile grill the red peppers, skin-side up, under a hot grill until blistered and charred. Place in a covered bowl and leave for 5 minutes, then peel away the skins. Slice the pepper flesh into fine julienne.

3 Toss the peppers with the cooked onions to serve.

Roast Winter Vegetables

30 ml (2 tbsp) sunflower oil
¼ swede, cut into 4 slices
4 baby carrots
4 celery sticks, cut into 5 cm (2 inch) lengths
4-6 Brussel sprouts
4-6 baby onions
4 baby parsnips
salt and freshly ground black pepper

1 Preheat a large ovenproof frying pan until hot, then add the sunflower oil. Add the vegetables (see note) and fry for about 5-6 minutes until well coloured, turning them once.

2 Season with salt and pepper, then pour on enough cold water to just cover the vegetables. Bring to the boil and cook until the liquid is reduced by two thirds.

3 Transfer the pan to a preheated oven at 220°C (425°F) mark 7 and cook for about 12 minutes until the vegetables are just tender.

Note: When frying the vegetables, avoid overcrowding the pan; if necessary cook in two batches.

Spiced Sweet Potato Purée

450 g (1 lb) sweet potatoes, peeled and cut into even-sized chunks
450 g (1 lb) waxy red potatoes, peeled and diced
75 g (3 oz) butter
15-30 ml (1-2 tbsp) soft brown sugar
finely grated zest of ½ orange
pinch of ground cinnamon
pinch of freshly grated nutmeg
30-60 ml (2-4 tbsp) whipping cream
30 ml (2 tbsp) balsamic vinegar (optional)
salt and freshly ground black pepper

1 Cook the potatoes separately in salted water until tender.

2 Drain thoroughly, return to the pan and dry over a low heat for a minute or two.

3 Put both potatoes through a potato ricer back into one warm pan. Add the remaining ingredients, seasoning with salt and pepper to taste. Mix well and turn into a warmed serving dish.

Potato and Parsnip Cakes

2 medium red potatoes
4 small parsnips
1 egg yolk, beaten
salt and freshly ground black pepper
olive oil, for frying

1 Peel and grate the potatoes and parsnips, discarding the parsnip cores. Place in a clean tea-towel and wring to squeeze out any excess liquid; do not rinse.

2 Put the grated potatoes and parsnips into a bowl. Mix in the beaten egg yolk and season with salt and pepper.

3 Heat a thin film of olive oil in a heavy-based frying pan until almost smoking. Lightly oil four 7.5 cm (3 inch) metal rings and place in the pan. Spoon enough potato mixture into each one to make a cake approximately 1 cm (½ inch) thick, pressing down firmly.

4 Fry for about 4 minutes, then carefully remove the rings. Continue to cook for a further 1 minute or so, until the underside is crisp and browned, carefully checking by lifting the cake with a palette knife.

5 Turn the cakes over and cook the other side for 5 minutes, again until nicely browned. Remove from the pan and drain on kitchen paper. Serve piping hot.

Note: These cakes can be prepared in advance and reheated on a baking sheet in a medium oven for about 15-20 minutes.

Parsnip and Carrot Cakes

225 g (8 oz) peeled parsnips
110 g (4 oz) peeled carrots
salt and freshly ground black pepper
30 ml (2 tbsp) plain flour
30 ml (2 tbsp) melted butter
pinch of ground mace
butter, for frying

1 Coarsely shred or grate the parsnips and carrots, using a food processor or grater. Blanch in boiling salted water for 1-2 minutes until cooked but still firm to the bite. Drain thoroughly and allow to cool.

2 When cold, sift in the flour and mix carefully with a fork so as not to break up or mash the vegetables. Add the melted butter and carefully fork through, then season with the mace, salt and pepper.

3 Divide the mixture between four 11 cm (4½ inch) loose-bottomed flan tins base-lined with a disc of non-stick baking parchment. Chill in the refrigerator for about 45 minutes to cool and firm up.

4 When ready to cook, melt a little butter in a small frying pan. Invert one of the cakes into the pan, removing the flan ring and base. Fry gently for 5 minutes on each side until golden and crisp. Remove and drain on kitchen paper. Keep warm in a low oven while frying the other 3 cakes, adding more butter to the pan as necessary. Serve piping hot.

Clapshot

600 g (1 lb 5 oz) floury potatoes, peeled and
chopped
½ medium swede, peeled and chopped
salt and freshly ground black pepper
30 ml (2 tbsp) double cream
60 g (2½ oz) unsalted butter
freshly grated nutmeg

1 Add the potatoes and swede to a pan of cold salted water. Bring to the boil and cook until tender. Drain well and pass through a potato ricer into a warm bowl.

2 Heat the cream and butter together and beat into the potato and swede mixture. Season with salt, pepper and nutmeg to taste. Serve piping hot.

Neeps and Tatties

450 g (1 lb) swedes
450 g (1 lb) potatoes
1 carrot
salt and freshly ground black pepper
100 g (4 oz) butter

1 Peel the vegetables and cut into even-sized pieces. Cook in boiling salted water until tender.

2 Drain the vegetables and return to the pan. Mash with a potato masher, adding the butter and seasoning with salt and pepper to taste. Serve piping hot.

Potato and Spinach Galette

450 g (1 lb) potatoes, peeled
225 g (8 oz) spinach leaves
salt and freshly ground black pepper
1 egg
pinch of freshly grated nutmeg
salt and freshly ground black pepper
groundnut oil, for frying

1 Finely grate the potatoes and squeeze out any surplus liquid. Place in a bowl.

2 Cook the spinach in a pan with just the water clinging to the leaves after washing for about 1 minute until wilted. Drain thoroughly, pressing to extract all water, then finely chop the spinach.

3 Season the grated potato with salt and pepper, add the egg and mix well. Grease four 7.5 cm (3 inch) metal cutters and place on a tray. Divide half of the potato between the cutters and press well down. Cover with the spinach, seasoning lightly with nutmeg. Top with the rest of the grated potato and press down.

5 Heat a thin film of groundnut oil in a heavy-based frying pan. Lift the galettes into the hot pan and fry gently for about 5 minutes on each side until golden. Drain on kitchen paper and serve.

Sweet Potato Purée

700 g (1½ lb) sweet potatoes
salt and freshly ground black pepper
60 ml (2 fl oz) double cream
50 g (2 oz) butter

1 Peel the sweet potatoes and cut into even-sized chunks. Add to a pan of salted water, bring to the boil and cook until tender.

2 Drain thoroughly, then mash with plenty of pepper and salt to taste. Add the cream and butter; mash until smooth.

3 Spoon the sweet potato purée into warmed greased dariole moulds.

4 When ready to serve, reheat in a hot oven for about 5 minutes. Turn out onto warm plates to serve.

Potato and Celeriac Julienne

4 large baking potatoes
1 medium celeriac
30 ml (2 tbsp) olive oil
2.5 ml (½ tsp) thyme
salt and freshly ground black pepper

1 Peel the potatoes and celeriac and trim to squares. Cut both into julienne and blanch in boiling water for 2-3 minutes. Drain thoroughly and pat dry with kitchen paper.

2 Toss the julienne with the olive oil, thyme, salt and pepper. Spread out in a shallow baking tin and cook in a preheated oven at 190°C (375°F) mark 5 for 20-30 minutes until tender and golden brown. Serve piping hot.

Pan-fried Potato and Celeriac Pancake

450 g (1 lb) potatoes
450 g (1 lb) celeriac
1 clove garlic, peeled
salt and freshly ground black pepper

1 Peel the potatoes and celeriac and cut into large even-sized chunks. Add to a pan of salted water with the garlic, bring to the boil, cover and simmer for about 20 minutes until tender. Drain thoroughly and return to the pan. Place over a low heat for 2-3 minutes, stirring frequently, to dry out.

2 Mash thoroughly and briefly work with a hand blender if available – for a smoother texture. Season with salt and pepper to taste.

3 Shape the mixture into 4 flat cakes, each about 11 cm (4½ inches) in diameter and 2 cm (¾ inch) thick. Place on an oiled baking tray. Bake in a preheated oven at 200°C (400°F) mark 6 for about 20 minutes until the bases are sufficiently crisp for the pancakes to be lifted cleanly. Trim the pancakes to neat rounds, using a 10 cm (4 inch) metal cutter.

4 Transfer to a hot dry frying pan and fry for 2-3 minutes on each side until golden and crisp. Serve piping hot.

Parsnip and Potato Rösti

450 g (1 lb) potatoes, peeled
450 g (1 lb) parsnip, peeled and cored
125 g (4 oz) unsalted butter, melted
freshly grated nutmeg, to taste
salt and freshly ground black pepper

1 Coarsely grate the potatoes and parsnips, place on a tea-towel and wring to remove as much moisture as possible.

2 Transfer to a bowl and add half of the melted butter, nutmeg, salt and pepper to taste. Pack into 9 cm (3½ inch) metal rings, placed on a tray. Chill in the refrigerator for 30 minutes.

3 Heat the remaining butter in a frying pan, add the rösti and fry for 2-3 minutes on each side until lightly golden. Carefully transfer to a baking tray.

4 Remove the rings and bake in a preheated oven at 200°C (400°F) mark 6 for 20-25 minutes. Serve piping hot.

Butter-basted Potatoes

25 g (1 oz) butter
24 small even-sized new potatoes
salt and freshly ground black pepper

1 Melt the butter in a heavy-based pan (that will accommodate all the potatoes in one layer), then add the potatoes. Cover and shake the pan once or twice.

2 Leave to cook on a gentle heat for 20-25 minutes, shaking the pan occasionally to make sure the potatoes don't stick. When cooked, drain, season with salt and pepper to taste and serve.

Gingered Potato and Parsnip Cakes

400 g (14 oz) potatoes, peeled and chopped
250 g (9 oz) parsnips, peeled and chopped
30 g (1 oz) unsalted butter
30 g (1 oz) Parmesan cheese, freshly grated
15 g (½ oz) fresh root ginger, peeled and finely grated
salt and freshly ground black pepper
plain flour, for coating
30-45 ml (2-3 tbsp) groundnut oil

1 Cook the potatoes and parsnips in boiling salted water until soft. Drain, then mash with the butter, cheese and ginger. Season with salt and pepper to taste. Leave to cool to room temperature.

2 Shape the mixture into 12 small balls, then roll in the flour to coat and flatten into small cakes.

3 Heat the oil in a frying pan, add the cakes and fry for 4-5 minutes each side until crisp and golden. Drain on kitchen paper and serve hot.

Note: These cakes can be prepared in advance if required and reheated in a hot oven for 5 minutes.

Potato Galette

2 large baking potatoes
salt and freshly ground black pepper
85 ml (6 tbsp) melted clarified butter

1 Peel and halve the potatoes. Press a 7.5 cm (3 inch) metal cutter into each potato half to shape into a neat cylinder. Finely slice each potato cylinder.

2 Blanch the potato slices in boiling water for about 3 minutes. Remove and pat dry on a clean tea-towel. Season with salt and pepper.

3 Divide the melted butter between 4 ramekins, then fill with the potato slices, pressing them neatly in layers.

4 Bake in a preheated oven at 230°C (450°F) mark 8 for 20 minutes until golden brown on top and soft in the centre. Serve piping hot.

Potato Purée

700 g (1½ lb) potatoes, peeled and cut into
even-sized pieces
100 g (4 oz) unsalted butter, softened
salt and freshly ground white pepper

1 Add the potatoes to a pan of salted water, bring to the boil, cover and simmer for about 20-30 minutes until tender. Drain thoroughly and return to the pan. Place over a low heat for a few minutes to dry out.

2 Pass the potatoes through a vegetable mill or sieve into a warm bowl. Beat in the butter and season with salt and pepper to taste. Serve at once.

Potatoes Anna

6 medium/large potatoes (preferably King
Edward's)
350 g (12 oz) butter, melted
(approximately)
sea salt and freshly ground black pepper

1 Peel and thinly slice the potatoes; immerse in a bowl of cold water.

2 Stand four 9 cm (3½ inch) metal rings, each 4 cm (1½ inches) deep, on a baking sheet. Line with foil to form small metal containers. Brush generously with melted butter.

3 Drain the potatoes and pat dry. Layer the potatoes in the metal rings, covering each layer with butter and seasoning with salt and pepper. Fill the rings to the top, pushing down the potato slices if necessary.

4 Cook in a preheated oven at 220°C (425°F) mark 7 for 30 minutes or until the potatoes are tender, checking from time to time that they are not over-browning; if necessary cover with foil.

5 Loosen the potato cakes with a knife and unmould onto warmed serving plates.

Truffled Potatoes

24 new potatoes
salt and freshly ground black pepper
25 g (1 oz) butter
few drops of truffle oil

1 Cook the potatoes in boiling salted water until tender. Drain and toss with the butter.

2 Mash the potatoes lightly with a fork to crush them slightly. Drizzle with the truffle oil, check the seasoning and serve.

Olive Oil Mashed Potato

900 g (2 lb) potatoes (Desirée or King Edwards)
salt and freshly ground black pepper
120 ml (4 fl oz) fine quality extra-virgin olive oil

1 Peel the potatoes, cut into even-sized pieces and cook in boiling salted water until tender; drain thoroughly and turn into a warmed bowl.

2 Using an electric hand whisk on low speed, begin to break up the potatoes, gradually adding half of the olive oil. As soon as it is incorporated, add the rest of the olive oil and whisk until smooth and fluffy. Season well with salt and pepper. Serve piping hot.

Red Pesto Mashed Potato

1 large red pepper
150 ml (¼ pint) olive oil
50 g (2 oz) pine nuts
1 small clove garlic, crushed
1 large bunch of basil, stems removed
25 g (1 oz) Parmesan cheese, finely grated
450 g (1 lb) potatoes
salt and freshly ground black pepper
50 g (2 oz) unsalted butter
60 ml (2 fl oz) double cream

1 Brush the red pepper with olive oil and roast in a preheated oven at 200°C (400°F) mark 6 for about 40 minutes until the skin is charred. Place in a covered bowl until cool enough to handle, then remove the skin. Halve, core and deseed the pepper, then chop roughly.

2 Heat 30 ml (2 tbsp) of the olive oil in a frying pan, add the pine nuts and fry gently for 1-2 minutes until golden brown. Allow to cool.

3 Put the red pepper, garlic, torn basil leaves, Parmesan and seasoning in a blender with the cooled pine nuts and remaining olive oil. Work to a purée.

4 Cook the potatoes in boiling salted water for about 20 minutes until tender. Drain thoroughly and return to the pan. Shake hard to start to break the potatoes up. Add the butter and cream a little at a time. Gradually add the pesto until you reach the desired strength of flavour. Check the seasoning. Serve at once.

Pommes Mousseline with Chives

450 g (1 lb) floury potatoes, peeled and
    quartered
salt and freshly ground black pepper
50 g (2 oz) unsalted butter
60-120 ml (2-4 fl oz) cream of the milk or
    double cream
15 ml (1 tbsp) chopped chives
knob of butter
chives, to garnish

1 Line 4 oblong metal moulds, measuring
6 x 4 cm (2½ x 1½ inches) with foil. Brush
with melted butter.

2 Add the potatoes to a pan of salted
water, bring to the boil and cook for about
20 minutes until tender but not falling
apart.

3 Drain the potatoes and return to the
pan. Cover with the lid and shake over a
low heat to dry off any excess moisture.

4 Mash the potatoes and add the unsalted
butter and enough cream or creamy milk
to give a very light, creamy consistency,
beating with a wooden spoon. Check the
seasoning and add the chopped chives.

5 Spoon the potato into the moulds, level
the surface and top with a knob of butter.
Keep warm in the oven until required.

6 To serve, carefully turn out of the
moulds onto warmed plates, easing the foil
away. Garnish with chives.

Potato Rösti

2 large potatoes
salt and freshly ground black pepper
60 g (2½ oz) melted clarified butter

1 To make the potato rösti, grate the
potatoes into long strands, place on a clean
tea-towel and wring to squeeze out the
moisture. Turn into a bowl, season with
salt and pepper to taste and mix with the
clarified butter.

2 Place four 10 cm (4 inch) metal rings
on a baking tray lined with non-stick
baking parchment. Spoon a quarter of the
potato mixture into each ring and spread
evenly.

3 Bake in a preheated oven at 180°C
(350°F) mark 4 for 10 minutes until crisp.
Remove the metal rings. Serve piping hot.

Oven-rösti Potatoes

700 g (1½ lb) medium potatoes
1 small onion or 2 shallots, finely chopped
45 ml (3 tbsp) chopped parsley
salt and freshly ground black pepper
50 g (2 oz) butter, melted

1 Add the potatoes to a pan of boiling
salted water and par-boil for 10 minutes;
drain and leave to cool.

2 Grate the cooled potatoes, using a coarse
grater, and place in a bowl. Add the onion,
parsley and seasoning; mix well.

3 Lightly butter 8 patty tins and press the
mixture into them. Pour over the melted
butter and cook in a preheated oven at
190°C (375°F) mark 5 for 1 hour until
golden and tender.

Saffron Rice

1.25 ml (½ tsp) saffron strands
350 ml (12 fl oz) boiling water
250 g (9 oz) Basmati rice
salt

1 Put the saffron in a small bowl, pour on the boiling water and leave to infuse for 1 hour.

2 Wash the rice in cold water, then place in a saucepan. Pour on the saffron liquid, add salt and bring to the boil. Cover and simmer for 20 minutes or until just tender and the liquid is absorbed.

3 Lightly oil 4 timbales or other individual moulds and fill with the rice, packing it in firmly. Cover loosely with foil and keep warm until required.

4 To serve, unmould the timbales onto warmed plates and serve at once.

Arroz Blanco (Mexican White Rice)

175 g (6 oz/1 cup) basmati rice
1 clove garlic, peeled
1 green chilli
15 ml (1 tbsp) olive oil
15 g (½ oz) butter
1 onion, finely chopped
450 ml (¾ pint) chicken stock
pinch of salt

1 Rinse the rice thoroughly in cold water to remove excess starch; drain. Thread the garlic clove and green chilli onto a wooden cocktail stick.

2 Heat the oil and butter in a saucepan (that has a tight-fitting lid). Add the onion and sweat gently until softened but not coloured. Add the rice and stir well to coat all of the grains with butter.

3 Add the stock, garlic and chilli, and a pinch of salt. Bring to a simmer, cover the pan and reduce the heat to its lowest setting. Cook for 8-10 minutes until the liquid is absorbed and the rice is *al dente*. Discard the cocktail stick before serving.

Timbales of Basmati and Wild Rice with Chives

175 g (6 oz) Tilda mixed basmati and wild rice
40 g (1½ oz) butter
30 ml (2 tbsp) chopped chives
salt and freshly ground black pepper

1 Bring a large pan of water to the boil, add the rice, stir once, then cover and cook for 20 minutes; drain thoroughly.

2 Add the butter, chives and salt and pepper to taste; fork through. Press the rice into 4 buttered timbales or ramekins. Cover and keep warm for up to 30 minutes in a roasting tin half-filled with hot water.

3 To unmould, briefly dip the timbales into cold water and invert onto warmed serving plates.

Skirlie

75 ml (5 tbsp) olive oil or dripping
1 large onion, finely chopped
100 g (3½ oz) medium oatmeal
salt and freshly ground black pepper
30-45 ml (2-3 tbsp) finely chopped mixed parsley and chives

1 Heat the oil or dripping in a heavy-based frying pan, add the onion and fry gently until softened and turning golden.

2 Stir in the oatmeal and fry for about 10 minutes until crumbly and golden.

3 Season liberally with salt and pepper, sprinkle generously with the chopped herbs and serve.

Buttered Noodles

175 g (6 oz) plain flour
25 g (1 oz) fine semolina
2 eggs
pinch of salt
few drops of olive oil

1 Put the flour and semolina in a mound on a clean work surface and make a well in the centre. Break the eggs into the well and add a pinch of salt. Stir the eggs into the flour with a fork to begin with, then use your fingers to mix the ingredients to a firm dough. If the dough is too moist, work in some more flour.

2 Wrap the pasta dough in cling film and leave to rest in the refrigerator for 30 minutes.

3 Using a pasta machine, roll out the pasta to the required thickness. Fit the tagliatelle cutters and pass the pasta through to cut into noodles.

4 Add the pasta to a large pan of boiling water with the olive oil, stir once to prevent sticking, and boil for about 3 minutes until *al dente*. Drain and serve immediately.

Desserts

Pear Sponge Pudding with Brandy and Ginger Sauce, served with Cardamom Custard

150 g (5 oz) self-raising flour
pinch of salt
5 ml (1 tsp) baking powder
110 g (4 oz) butter, softened
110 g (4 oz) caster sugar
2 eggs (size 1)
1 medium pear
finely grated zest of 1 lemon

Sauce:
110 g (4 oz) unsalted butter
175 g (6 oz) soft brown sugar
60 ml (4 tbsp) ginger wine
30 ml (2 tbsp) brandy
2 pieces preserved stem ginger in syrup,
   drained and finely chopped

Cardamom Custard:
2 cardamom pods
150 ml (¼ pint) milk
150 ml (¼ pint) double cream
½ bay leaf
4 egg yolks
40 g (1½ oz) caster sugar

1 First make the sauce. Heat the butter and brown sugar together in a small pan over a low heat until the sugar is dissolved, then whisk in the ginger wine and brandy. Add the chopped stem ginger, then set aside to cool.

2 To make the puddings, butter four 175 ml (6 fl oz) individual pudding basins (see note). Sift the flour, salt and baking powder into a large bowl. Add the softened butter, caster sugar and eggs and whisk thoroughly, using an electric hand whisk, until the mixture is smooth and creamy.

Peel, halve, core and finely chop the pear. Lightly fold the pear into the mixture, with the grated lemon zest.

3 Put 2 tablespoons of the ginger sauce into each pudding basin and spoon the pudding mixture on top, leaving about a 1 cm (½ inch) margin at the top to allow the pudding to rise. Smooth the surface with the back of the spoon. Place a square of foil on top of each pudding, making a pleat in the centre, then fold in the edges of the foil all the way around the edge of the basin to seal.

4 Place the puddings in a steamer, cover tightly and steam for 1 hour, topping up with boiling water during cooking if necessary.

5 To make the cardamom custard, split the cardamom pods open, extract the seeds and gently crush them. Place in a saucepan with the milk, cream and bay leaf. Slowly bring to the boil. Meanwhile, beat the egg yolks and sugar together in a heatproof bowl until well blended. Place the bowl over a pan of simmering water and pour on the hot cream mixture, whisking all the time. Stir until the custard thickens enough to coat the back of a wooden spoon. Remove the bowl from the heat.

6 Allow the puddings to stand for 10-15 minutes before turning out onto individual serving plates. Drizzle the rest of the warmed ginger sauce over the puddings and serve with the cardamom custard.

Note: If preferred make one large pudding in a 1 litre (1¾ pint) pudding basin. Steam for 2½ hours.

Individual Lemon Bread and Butter Pudding with a Sabayon Sauce

handful of raisins
juice of 1 lemon
500 ml (16 fl oz) double cream
50 g (2 oz) caster sugar
1 vanilla pod
grated zest of 2 lemons
½ loaf open-textured white bread
  (eg Bloomer)
100 g (3½ oz) butter, softened
6 egg yolks

Sabayon:
4 egg yolks
50 g (2 oz) caster sugar
150 ml (¼ pint) dry white wine

Caramel Topping:
20 ml (4 tsp) caster sugar

To Decorate:
lemon balm or mint sprigs

1 To make the puddings, soak the raisins in the lemon juice for 30 minutes - 1 hour. Put the cream, sugar, vanilla pod and lemon zest in a saucepan and slowly bring to the boil, stirring occasionally. Turn off the heat and leave to infuse for 20-30 minutes with the lid on.

2 Generously butter the inside of 4 ramekins. Slice the bread as thinly as possible – the slices should be no more than 5 mm (¼ inch) thick. Butter generously on one side only. Using a pastry cutter, cut 4 rounds of bread – to fit in the bottom of each ramekin. Place the bread rounds butter-side down in the ramekins.

3 For the sides cut 4 strips, a little wider than the depth of the ramekins. Place butter-side outwards around the side of each ramekin, overlapping the ends slightly. Ensure the bottom edge meets the bread round and allow the top edge to stand slightly proud of the rim.

4 Beat the egg yolks together in a bowl. Strain the lemon-cream mixture onto the egg yolks, whisking constantly, until evenly combined, and smooth. Pour into each ramekin almost to the top. Drain the raisins and scatter about six into each custard. Cover loosely with buttered foil and leave to rest in a roasting tin for at least 30 minutes – 1 hour.

5 Place the ramekins in a large steamer (or on a trivet in a large saucepan over simmering water), and steam gently for 40-50 minutes. Remove the ramekins and keep warm until ready to turn out.

6 To make the sabayon, whisk the egg yolks and sugar together in a heatproof bowl over a pan of simmering water (making sure that the bowl never comes into contact with the water) until the mixture is pale, frothy and at least doubled in volume. Add the wine, a little at a time, whisking constantly until a pale, light and frothy sabayon is obtained.

7 To assemble, trim the excess bread from the rim of each pudding, slide a thin-bladed knife down around the side and carefully turn out onto the centre of a warmed flameproof serving plate. Sprinkle the top of each pudding evenly with caster sugar and place under a preheated hot grill until caramelised. (Alternatively, use a blow torch.) Leave to cool for a few minutes until the caramel is hardened.

8 Spoon the sabayon sauce around the puddings and decorate with lemon balm or mint to serve.

Lemon and Lime Sponge with Lemon Custard Sauce

75 g (3 oz) unsalted butter
100 g (4 oz) caster sugar
3 eggs (size 1), separated
50 g (2 oz) self-raising flour, sifted
juice and grated zest of 3 limes
juice and grated zest of 1 lemon
300 ml (½ pint) milk

Lemon Custard Sauce:
150 ml (¼ pint) full-fat milk
150 ml (¼ pint) double cream
1 vanilla pod, split
finely pared zest of 1 lemon
4 egg yolks
40 g (1½ oz) caster sugar

1 Beat the butter and sugar together in a bowl until pale and creamy. Beat the egg yolks together, then gradually beat into the creamed mixture. Fold in the flour, citrus zests and juices, alternating with the milk.

2 In another bowl, whisk the egg whites until they form soft peaks, then fold into the sponge mixture. Divide the mixture between 4-6 well-buttered ramekins or individual pudding mounds. Bake in a preheated oven at 170°C (325°F) mark 3 for 50 minutes until the tops are golden.

3 Meanwhile, make the custard. Pour the milk and cream into a saucepan. Scrape out the seeds from the vanilla pod and add to the pan with the lemon zest. Slowly bring to the boil. Meanwhile, beat the egg yolks and sugar together in a heatproof bowl. Place the bowl over a pan of simmering water and whisk in the hot cream mixture. Stir until the custard is thick enough to coat the back of a wooden spoon. Strain through a sieve into a serving jug to remove the lemon zest.

4 When cooked, leave the puddings in their moulds for a few minutes, then run a knife around the edge of each one to loosen it. Carefully turn out onto warmed serving plates and serve with the lemon custard sauce.

Vanilla Sponge Pudding with Kahlua Anglaise

120 g (4 oz) butter, softened
120 g (4 oz) caster sugar
2 eggs (size 3), beaten
120 g (4 oz) self-raising flour
60-90 ml (4-6 tbsp) milk (approximately)
2 vanilla pods, split

Kahlua Anglaise:
300 ml (½ pint) milk
50-75 g (2-3 oz) caster sugar
4 egg yolks
15-30 ml (1-2 tbsp) kahlua, or other coffee
   liqueur

To Finish:
chocolate shavings

1 Cream the butter and sugar together in a bowl. Gradually beat in the eggs, a little at a time. Fold in the flour, using a large metal spoon. Add sufficient milk to give a dropping consistency. Extract the seeds from the vanilla pods, then fold into the mixture. (Reserve the pods for the sauce.)

2 Divide the mixture between four 150 ml (¼ pint) individual moulds and cover with pleated discs of foil. Cook in a steamer over boiling water for 40 minutes, or until well risen and a skewer inserted into the centre comes out clean. Remove from the steamer and let cool slightly.

3 To make the kahlua anglaise, pour the milk into a heavy-based pan and add the empty vanilla pods and 15 ml (1 tbsp) of the sugar. Slowly bring to the boil. Meanwhile, whisk the egg yolks and remaining sugar together in a bowl until pale and creamy. Pour on the hot milk, whisking all the time. Return to the pan and stir over a low heat until thickened enough to coat the back of the wooden spoon. Stir in the kahlua, to taste.

4 To serve, turn out each pudding onto a warmed serving plate and pour the sauce around. Scatter the chocolate shavings on top of the puddings and serve warm.

Chocolate Saveur with Orange and Passion Fruit Sauce

Saveur:
115 g (4 oz) fine quality plain dark
  chocolate, in pieces
50 g (2 oz) unsalted butter
30 g (1¼ oz) ground almonds
40 g (1½ oz) rice flour, sifted
60 ml (4 tbsp) milk
2 eggs, separated
90 g (3½ oz) caster sugar

Orange and Passion Fruit Sauce:
500 ml (16 fl oz) orange juice
3 passion fruit
25 g (1 oz) cornflour, mixed with 30 ml
  (2 tbsp) orange juice
100 g (3½ oz) caster sugar
120 ml (4 fl oz) water

Chocolate Sauce:
115 g (4 oz) fine quality plain dark
  chocolate, in pieces
75 ml (5 tbsp) milk

To Serve:
cocoa powder, for dusting

1 Grease four 5.5 cm (2½ inch) individual tins (see note) and line with greaseproof paper, to stand about 6 cm (2½ inches) high.

2 To make the saveur, melt the chocolate in a bowl set over a pan of simmering water. Stir in the butter and ground almonds and let cool slightly. Put the flour into a bowl and stir in the milk, mixing until smooth. Stir in the egg yolks.

3 In a clean bowl, whisk the egg whites to soft peaks. Gradually whisk in the sugar, a spoonful at a time. Continue to whisk until the meringue is firm and glossy.

4 Stir the chocolate mixture into the flour mixture, then fold in a spoonful of the meringue to lighten the mixture. Carefully fold in the remaining meringue, using a large metal spoon.

5 Spoon the mixture into the prepared moulds, to three-quarters fill them. Stand on a baking tray and cook in a preheated oven at 180°C (350°F) mark 4 for 30-35 minutes.

6 Meanwhile, make the orange and passion fruit sauce. Bring the orange juice to the boil in a saucepan and boil rapidly until reduced to 200 ml (7 fl oz). Halve the passion fruit, scoop out the flesh and seeds into a sieve over a bowl and press to extract the juice. Stir the passion fruit juice into the orange juice, with the blended cornflour and cook, stirring, for 1-2 minutes until thickened and smooth.

7 Dissolve the sugar in the water, in a separate pan, then bring to the boil. Add this sugar syrup to the orange and passion fruit sauce, a little at a time, until you have a pouring consistency.

8 To make the chocolate sauce, melt the chocolate and milk together in a bowl over a pan of simmering water, stirring until smooth. Set aside; keep warm.

9 Once the saveurs are cooked, carefully unmould and cut off the tops, using a sharp knife. Gently hollow out the middle of each saveur to form a well, then pour in the chocolate sauce. Replace the tops, dust with cocoa powder and place on serving plates. Surround with the warm orange and passion fruit sauce and serve at once.

Note: If small individual cake tins are unobtainable, use small empty cans (eg evaporated milk cans), or line metal rings with foil to form containers.

Individual Rhubarb and Ginger Crumbles with an Orange Sauce

Pastry:
175 g (6 oz) self-raising flour
50 g (2 oz) cornflour
175 g (6 oz) butter, in pieces
50 g (2 oz) caster sugar
finely grated zest of ½ orange
1 large egg (size 1), beaten

Rhubarb Filling:
450 g (1 lb) young rhubarb, trimmed
three 1 cm (½ inch) cubes of fresh root ginger
15 ml (1 tbsp) caster sugar
15 ml (1 tbsp) water

Crumble Mix:
75 g (3 oz) plain flour
40 g (1½ oz) unsalted butter
40 g (1½ oz) caster sugar

Orange Sauce:
600 ml (1 pint) freshly squeezed orange juice
15 ml (1 tbsp) arrowroot
15 ml (1 tbsp) caster sugar, or to taste

To Serve:
crème fraîche

1 To make the pastry, sift the flour and cornflour into a bowl and rub in the butter until the mixture resembles breadcrumbs; do not overwork. Stir in the sugar and orange zest, then mix in the egg to form a soft dough. Wrap in cling film and leave to rest in the refrigerator for at least 4 hours.

2 Return the pastry to room temperature and roll out half on a lightly floured surface to a 5 mm (¼ inch) thickness. Use to line four 7.5 cm (3 inch) flan rings placed on a baking tray, easing the pastry to fit; leave a little excess pastry overhanging the edge of the rings. Refrigerate for 30 minutes. (Use the rest of the pastry for another occasion.)

3 Meanwhile, make the filling. Cut the rhubarb into 2.5 cm (1 inch) chunks. Place in a saucepan with the cubes of ginger, sugar and 15 ml (1 tbsp) water. Cook gently for about 5 minutes until the rhubarb is tender, but not broken up. Transfer to a bowl and leave to infuse for at least 1 hour.

4 In the meantime, line the pastry cases with foil and baking beans and bake blind in a preheated oven at 170°C (325°F) mark 3 for 30 minutes. Let cool, then trim the excess pastry from the top edge of the flans with a sharp knife. Increase the oven temperature to 200°C (400°F) mark 6.

5 To make the orange sauce, bring the orange juice to the boil in a saucepan and reduce by half, then remove from the heat. Mix the arrowroot to a smooth paste with 15 ml (1 tbsp) water. Gradually stir into the sauce, return to the heat and simmer gently, stirring constantly until the sauce is thick enough to lightly coat the back of the spoon. Sweeten with the sugar to taste, stirring to dissolve.

6 To prepare the crumble, sift the flour into a bowl and rub in the butter until the mixture resembles fine breadcrumbs. Add the sugar and mix lightly.

7 Remove the chunks of ginger from the rhubarb then fill the pastry cases with the rhubarb to just below the rims. Sprinkle the crumble over the rhubarb filling to cover completely. Bake in the oven for 15-20 minutes until the crumble is golden.

8 To serve, carefully unmould a crumble onto the centre of each warmed serving plate. Surround with the orange sauce and serve at once, with crème fraîche.

Poached Stuffed Pears on a Lace Coconut Pancake with Chocolate Sauce

Pancakes:
50 g (2 oz) plain flour
1 egg (size 3)
5 ml (1 tsp) ground ginger
120 ml (4 fl oz) coconut milk
a little oil, for frying

Pears:
750 ml (1½ pints) water
125 g (4 oz) sugar
15 ml (1 tbsp) vanilla extract
4 ripe pears

Stuffing:
75 g (3 oz) ricotta cheese
8 large amaretti biscuits, crushed
15 ml (1 tbsp) amaretto liqueur
15 ml (1 tbsp) crème fraîche
few drops of almond essence

Chocolate Sauce:
125 g (4 oz) plain chocolate, in pieces
15 ml (1 tbsp) single or double cream
15 ml (1 tbsp) amaretto liqueur

To Finish:
icing sugar, for dusting

1 First make the pancake batter. Put the flour, egg, ginger and coconut milk in a blender or food processor and work to a smooth batter. Transfer to a bowl, cover and leave to rest for 1 hour.

2 Put the water, sugar and vanilla extract in a saucepan over a low heat until the sugar is dissolved, then bring to a simmer. Meanwhile, peel the pears, leaving them whole and scoop out the core from the base of each one. Add the pears to the syrup and simmer for 10-20 minutes depending on ripeness, or until almost tender.

3 To make the sauce, melt the chocolate with the cream and liqueur in a heatproof bowl over a pan of simmering water. Stir until smooth.

4 In the meantime, mix together the ingredients for the stuffing until evenly combined. Lift the pears out of the syrup using a slotted spoon and fill with the stuffing. Put the pears into a small baking dish, moisten with a little of the syrup, cover and cook in a preheated oven at 200°C (400°F) mark 6 for 5-10 minutes until the filling is warmed through.

5 Meanwhile, cook the pancakes. Oil a heavy-based frying pan and heat until almost smoking. Using a piping bag fitted with a 5 mm (¼ inch) plain nozzle, quickly pipe some batter over the base of the pan to obtain a 10-12 cm (4-5 inch) pancake with a lacy effect. As soon as it is set, turn over and cook the other side. Remove and keep warm. Repeat to make 4 pancakes in total.

6 Lay a pancake on each warmed serving plate and position a stuffed pear on top. Using a piping bag, fitted with a fine writing nozzle, drizzle the chocolate sauce over the top. Dust with icing sugar and serve at once.

Butter Pecan Pancakes with Coffee and Chocolate Sauce, and Vanilla Ice Cream

Pancake Batter:
110 g (4 oz) plain flour
pinch of salt
2 eggs
300 ml (½ pint) milk

Filling:
75 g (3 oz) unsalted butter
25 g (1 oz) icing sugar
50 g (2 oz) pecan nuts, chopped

Ice Cream:
150 ml (¼ pint) double cream
150 ml (¼ pint) milk
½ vanilla pod, split
3 egg yolks
50 g (2 oz) caster sugar

Sauce:
10 ml (2 tsp) instant coffee granules
5 ml (1 tsp) hot water
40 g (1½ oz) unsalted butter
110 g (4 oz) white chocolate
15 g (½ oz) icing sugar, sifted
90 ml (6 tbsp) double cream

1 First make the ice cream. Pour the cream and milk into a heavy-based pan and heat slowly until almost boiling. Take off the heat. Scrape the seeds out of the vanilla pod and add them to the milk and cream with the pod. Stir, then cover and leave to infuse for 20 minutes. Whisk the egg yolks and sugar in a bowl until thick and creamy. Strain the milk and cream and pour onto the egg mixture, whisking continuously. Return to the pan and heat gently, stirring constantly, until thickened enough to coat the back of the wooden spoon; do not allow to boil. Pour into an ice-cream maker and churn until frozen.

2 To make the pancake batter, sift the flour and salt into a bowl, make a well in the middle and add the eggs. Gradually whisk the flour into the eggs, slowly adding the milk at the same time, to achieve a smooth batter; set aside.

3 To make the filling, in a bowl beat the butter and icing sugar together, then stir in the pecans; set aside.

4 To make the sauce, dissolve the coffee granules in the hot water; let cool. Melt the butter and chocolate together in a heat-proof bowl over a pan of simmering water. Remove from the heat and stir in the icing sugar, cream and coffee. Place in a heavy-based pan over a low heat and stir until smooth; do not boil. Keep warm.

5 To cook the pancakes, heat a crêpe pan until it is very hot, then grease with a little oil. Pour in about 30 ml (2 tbsp) batter, quickly swirling it around the pan to thinly cover the base. As soon as it sets, turn over and cook the other side. Transfer to a warmed plate and repeat until all the batter is used up. Depending on the size of the pan you should make 8-12 pancakes; stack them interleaved with greaseproof paper to prevent sticking.

6 To assemble, spread a little filling on each pancake and fold to enclose. Keep warm in a low oven until ready to serve.

7 To serve, arrange 2 or 3 pancakes on each warmed serving plate. Pour on a little sauce and add a scoop of ice cream. Serve immediately.

Note: The sauce is sufficient to serve 8, but it isn't practical to make a smaller amount. Use the rest for another occasion.

Warm Chocolate Tart with Pistachio Ice Cream

Pastry:
100 g (3½ oz) plain flour, sifted
60 g (2¼ oz) butter, in pieces
20 g (¾ oz) caster sugar
7.5 ml (½ tbsp) beaten egg
15 ml (1 tbsp) iced water

Filling:
200 g (7 oz) dark bitter chocolate
   (preferably 70% cocoa solids), in pieces
60 ml (2 fl oz) milk
120 ml (4 fl oz) double cream
1 egg

Pistachio Ice Cream:
500 ml (16 fl oz) milk
150 g (5 oz) skinned pistachio nuts, finely
   ground
5 egg yolks
75 g (3 oz) caster sugar
100 ml (3½ fl oz) double cream

To Finish:
cocoa powder and icing sugar, for dusting
strawberry slices and mint leaves,
   to decorate

1 First make the ice cream. Slowly bring the milk to the boil in a heavy-based pan. Remove from the heat, add the ground nuts and leave to cool and infuse for as long as possible. Meanwhile, whisk the egg yolks and sugar together until pale, then pour on the infused milk mixture, whisking continuously. Return to the pan and cook over a low heat until the mixture is thick enough to lightly coat the back of the spoon. Strain into a chilled bowl and allow to cool. Finally, stir in the cream. Churn the mixture in an ice-cream maker until frozen.

2 To make the pastry, put the flour and butter into a food processor and process briefly until the mixture resembles breadcrumbs. Add the sugar, egg and water and process until the dough forms a ball; do not over-mix. Wrap in cling film and chill in the refrigerator for 30 minutes.

3 Roll out the pastry thinly and use to line four 10 cm (4 inch) loose-bottomed flan tins. Chill in the refrigerator for 30 minutes.

4 Line the pastry cases with greaseproof paper and baking beans and bake blind in a preheated oven at 200°C (400°F) mark 6 for 12-15 minutes. Remove the paper and beans and return to the oven for a further 3-5 minutes until the base is cooked. Reduce the oven setting to 190°C (375°F) mark 5.

5 For the filling, put the chocolate in a bowl. Heat the milk and cream until almost boiling, then slowly pour onto the chocolate, whisking constantly until smooth. Let cool slightly.

6 Whisk the egg in another bowl, then add to the chocolate mixture and whisk until smooth.

7 Pour the chocolate mixture into the pastry cases, filling them to within a fraction of the rim. Bake in the oven for 20 minutes. Leave in the tins to cool slightly until warm.

8 To serve, carefully turn out each tart and dust lightly with cocoa powder, then icing sugar. Place a warm tart in the centre of each serving plate and a quenelle of ice cream next to it. Decorate with strawberry slices and mint leaves. Serve at once.

Banana Tarte Tatin with Coconut Ice Cream

Banana Tarte Tatin:
60 g (2¼ oz) unsalted butter
190 g (7 oz) caster sugar
40 ml (2½ tbsp) boiling water
4 large ripe bananas, chopped
250 g (9 oz) packet puff pastry

Coconut Ice Cream:
5 egg yolks (size 0)
40 g (1½ oz) caster sugar
15 ml (1 tbsp) honey
200 ml (7 fl oz) milk
70 g (2½ oz) creamed coconut, roughly
  chopped
300 ml (½ pint) double cream
30 ml (2 tbsp) dark rum

To Decorate:
4 physalis fruit

1 First make the ice cream. Beat the egg yolks, sugar and honey together in a bowl, then add the milk and creamed coconut. Pour into a heatproof bowl over a pan of simmering water and cook, stirring, until the mixture is thick enough to coat the back of a wooden spoon. Remove from the heat, pass through a sieve into a chilled bowl and allow to cool, then chill.

2 Stir the cream into the cold custard and add the rum. Transfer to an ice-cream maker and churn until thick. Transfer to a suitable container and store in the freezer until required.

3 To make the tarte tatin, melt the butter and sugar together in a heavy-based pan over a low heat, stirring occasionally until the mixture forms a golden caramel.

4 At this stage, dip the physalis fruit into the caramel and turn to coat, then set

aside. Protecting your hand with an oven glove, carefully add the boiling water to the remaining caramel, stirring constantly. Boil for 2 minutes, then strain. Allow to cool to room temperature.

5 To assemble the tarte tatins, place 4 metal rings, each 9 cm (3½ inches) in diameter and 3 cm (1¼ inches) deep on a baking sheet. Line the base and sides with foil, thus forming foil-based moulds. Coat the base of each mould with some of the caramel mixture, then arrange a single layer of bananas on top. Cover with the remaining caramel and form a second banana layer on top.

6 Roll out the puff pastry thinly on a lightly floured surface and cut out four 11 cm (4½ inch) rounds. Place on top of the bananas and press down firmly. Tuck the excess pastry down the sides of the tins. Chill in the refrigerator for 30 minutes.

7 Cook the tarte tatins in a preheated oven at 220°C (425°F) mark 7 for about 20 minutes until the pastry is crisp and golden brown. Allow to cool slightly before turning out onto serving plates.

8 Serve with a scoop of coconut ice cream and decorate with the caramel-coated physalis fruit.

Pear Tarte Tatin with Lemon Thyme Ice Cream

Pastry:
175 g (6 oz) plain flour
150 g (5 oz) unsalted butter, in pieces
50 g (2 oz) caster sugar
50 g (2 oz) ground rice
1 egg, beaten

Filling:
6 firm, under-ripe pears
110 g (4 oz) unsalted butter
110 g (4 oz) sugar
finely grated zest of 1 lemon

Ice Cream:
150 ml (¼ pint) milk
300 ml (½ pint) double cream
15 g (½ oz) lemon thyme
1 vanilla pod, split and seeds extracted
4 egg yolks
110 g (4 oz) caster sugar

To Decorate:
lemon thyme sprigs

1 First make the ice cream. Put the milk and cream in a heavy-based saucepan with the lemon thyme and seeds from the vanilla pod. Bring slowly to the boil, then remove from the heat and leave to infuse for 30 minutes. Strain through a sieve to remove the thyme.

2 In a bowl, whisk the egg yolks and sugar together until pale and thick, then gradually pour on the strained milk mixture, whisking all the time. Return to the pan and cook, stirring, over a low heat until the custard is thick enough to coat the back of the wooden spoon.

3 Turn the custard into a chilled bowl. Allow to cool, then transfer to an ice-cream maker, and churn until frozen.

4 To make the pastry, put the flour and butter into a food processor and process briefly until the mixture resembles breadcrumbs. Add the sugar, ground rice and egg and process until the dough forms a ball; do not over-mix. Roll out the pastry on a board between two large sheets of greaseproof paper and chill in the refrigerator for 20 minutes.

5 Meanwhile, for the filling, peel the pears and halve lengthwise, retaining the stalks. Carefully scoop out the cores. Using a sharp knife, slice the pears crosswise very thinly, keeping the slices together in sequence.

6 Put the butter and sugar in a shallow ovenproof pan, about 25 cm (10 inches) in diameter, and place over a low heat until the butter is melted and the sugar dissolved. Carefully place the pears in the pan rounded-side down; they should fit snugly. Sprinkle with the lemon zest and cook over a high heat for about 5 minutes until the pears are lightly caramelised.

7 Meanwhile, cut a round from the pastry, slightly larger than the diameter of the pan. Lift the pastry over the pears, tucking the edge down the side of the pan. Bake in a preheated oven at 180°C (350°F) mark 4 for 30 minutes. Leave in the tin for 20 seconds, then carefully invert onto a plate and spoon any juices back into the tart.

8 Serve the pear tatin slightly warm, cut into wedges and accompanied by the ice cream. Decorate with lemon thyme.

Chocolate and Pear Sabayon Tart

Pastry:
150 g (5 oz) plain flour, sifted
30 g (1 oz) cocoa powder
115 g (3¾ oz) butter, in pieces
50 g (1¾ oz) caster sugar
1 egg yolk
30 ml (2 tbsp) iced water

Filling:
2 ripe William pears
120 g (4 oz) caster sugar
300 ml (½ pint) water

Sabayon Cream:
4 egg yolks
60 g (2 oz) caster sugar

To Finish:
caster sugar, for dusting
30 g (1 oz) good-quality bitter chocolate
icing sugar, for dusting

1 Lightly butter and flour 4 loose-bottomed 10 cm (4 inch) individual fluted flan tins and place in the refrigerator along with a baking sheet, to chill.

2 To make the pastry, sift the flour and cocoa together into the food processor bowl. Add the butter and pulse until the mixture resembles rough breadcrumbs. Turn into a bowl and stir in the sugar.

3 Lightly whisk the egg yolk with the water and gradually add to the pastry, mixing with a round-bladed knife until you have a soft dough which can be gathered into a ball, leaving the sides of the bowl clean. Wrap in cling film and rest in the refrigerator for 30 minutes.

4 Roll out the pastry on a lightly floured surface to a 3 mm (⅛ inch) thickness.

Using a saucer or small plate as a guide, cut out 4 rounds, large enough to line the flan tins. Lay these on the chilled baking sheet and chill in the refrigerator for about 10 minutes. Line the flan tins with the pastry rounds, pressing gently into the flutes; trim the edges.

5 Line the pastry cases with greaseproof paper and baking beans. Bake on the middle shelf of a preheated oven at 190°C (375°F) mark 5 for about 20 minutes. Remove the paper and beans and bake for a further 10 minutes to crisp the bases. Remove from the oven, leaving the baking sheet inside.

6 Peel the pears, leaving the stalks on, then halve lengthwise splitting the stalks. Put the sugar and water in a heavy-based medium pan and dissolve over a low heat. Bring to a simmer, add the pear halves and poach gently for 5-10 minutes; they must remain slightly firm.

7 To make the sabayon cream, whisk the egg yolks with the caster sugar in a bowl set over a pan of barely simmering water until pale, creamy and doubled in volume.

8 Remove the pears from their poaching liquid with a slotted spoon and pat dry with kitchen paper. Lay one half in each pastry case, flat-side down and score the rounded surface with a sharp knife. Pour the sabayon cream around the pears to come within 5 mm (¼ inch) of the pastry rim. Sprinkle the pears with caster sugar. Place on the hot baking sheet in the oven and bake for about 10 minutes, until a soft, brown crust forms on the sabayon.

9 Meanwhile, melt the chocolate in a bowl set over a pan of hot water. To serve, place a pear sabayon tart on each serving plate and drizzle over the melted chocolate. Dust with icing sugar and serve at once.

Pear and Ginger Crumble Tart with Almond Cream

Pastry:
100 g (4 oz) plain flour
40 g (1½ oz) icing sugar
pinch of salt
25 g (1 oz) ground almonds
50 g (2 oz) unsalted butter, chilled and
    diced
1 egg, beaten
25 ml (1 fl oz) milk

Crumble:
15 g (½ oz) plain flour
15 g (½ oz) ground almonds
15 ml (1 tbsp) muscovado sugar
15 g (½ oz) unsalted butter, chilled and
    diced

Filling:
2 hard under-ripe pears (preferably Rocha)
25 g (1 oz) unsalted butter
60 ml (4 tbsp) caster sugar (approximately)
1 piece preserved stem ginger in syrup, finely
    diced
15 ml (1 tbsp) ginger syrup (from the jar)
30 ml (2 tbsp) pear brandy

Almond Cream:
300 ml (½ pint) double cream
10-15 ml (2-3 tsp) almond extract
5-10 ml (1-2 tsp) icing sugar, to taste

To Decorate:
icing sugar, for dusting
mint sprigs, to decorate

1 To make the pastry, sift the flour, icing sugar, salt and ground almonds together into a bowl and stir to mix. Rub in the butter until the mixture resembles breadcrumbs. Beat the egg and milk together. Gradually mix this into the rubbed-in mixture, until a smooth dough is formed. Wrap in cling film and leave to rest in the refrigerator for 30 minutes.

2 Roll out the pastry thinly and use to line four 9 cm (3½ inch) individual loose-bottomed fluted flan tins (see note). Chill in the refrigerator while preparing the filling.

3 To make the crumble mixture, mix the flour, ground almonds and sugar together in a bowl. Rub in the butter until a crumble mixture is achieved.

4 To make the filling, peel, core and chop the pears into 2.5 cm (1 inch) cubes. Heat the butter and 15 ml (1 tbsp) of the caster sugar in a large heavy-based frying pan until very hot. Add the chopped pears and sprinkle with the remaining sugar. Cook for 15-20 minutes until the pears are slightly caramelised, adding a little more sugar if required. Towards the end of the cooking time, stir in the diced ginger and syrup. Add the brandy and flame if required. Drain off excess liquor if necessary – the filling needs to be quite dry.

5 Divide the pear and ginger filling between the flan cases and top with the crumble mixture. Cook in a preheated oven at 180°C (350°F) mark 4 for 15 minutes or until brown.

6 Meanwhile, prepare the almond cream. Lightly whisk the cream with the almond extract to a pouring consistency, then add icing sugar to taste.

7 To serve, place a crumble tart on each serving plate and surround with the almond cream. Dust with icing sugar and decorate with sprigs of mint.

Note: As this pastry is rich and quite difficult to roll out, you may find it easier to use your fingers to mould the pastry into the tins. The flan cases do not need to be baked blind.

Pear and Walnut Tarts with Caramel Sauce

Pastry:
150 g (5 oz) plain flour
1.25 ml (¼ tsp) salt
40 g (1½ oz) butter
25 g (1 oz) white vegetable fat
25 g (1 oz) ground walnuts
50 g (2 oz) caster sugar
1 egg yolk
22 ml (1½ tbsp) iced water

Filling:
50 g (2 oz) sugar
150 ml (¼ pint) water
2 large ripe pears

To Glaze:
1 egg white, lightly beaten
a little sugar

Caramel Sauce:
100 g (4 oz) sugar
60 ml (4 tbsp) water
300 ml (½ pint) double cream
25 g (1 oz) butter

1 To make the pastry, sift the flour and salt into a bowl and rub in the butter and vegetable fat until the mixture resembles fine breadcrumbs. Stir in the ground walnuts and sugar. Mix the egg yolk with the iced water. Add to the dry ingredients and mix to bind the dough. Wrap in cling film and chill in the refrigerator for about 30 minutes.

2 In the meantime, prepare the filling. Dissolve the sugar in the water in a medium pan over a low heat, then increase the heat and boil for 4-5 minutes.

3 Peel, halve and core the pears. Add to the syrup and simmer for 10-15 minutes until tender but still firm. Leave to cool.

4 Roll out half of the pastry and use to line 4 individual deep 7.5 cm (3 inch) loose-bottomed flan tins. Place one pear half in each pastry case and drizzle with a little of the syrup.

5 Roll out the remaining pastry and cut out 4 rounds to make lids. Brush the edges of the pastry cases with water, position the lids and press the edges together to seal well.

6 Brush the tops with egg white and sprinkle with a little sugar to glaze. Bake in a preheated oven at 190°C (375°F) mark 5 for 20-30 minutes until golden.

7 Meanwhile, make the sauce. Dissolve the sugar in the water in a small heavy-based pan over a low heat, then increase the heat and boil, without stirring, until a light caramel is achieved. Remove from the heat and carefully stir in the cream and butter, protecting your hand with a cloth as the mixture will splutter.

8 To serve, carefully remove the tarts from the tins and place on warmed plates. Serve with the caramel sauce.

Plum and Almond Tart with Plum Sauce

Almond Pastry:
50 g (2 oz) butter
52 g (2 oz) caster sugar
1 egg (size 3)
50 g (2 oz) ground almonds
125 g (4 oz) plain flour

Frangipan:
75 g (3 oz) butter
75 g (3 oz) sugar
25 g (1 oz) plain flour
75 g (3 oz) ground almonds
1 egg (size 3)

Filling and Sauce:
8 plums, halved and stoned
90 ml (3 fl oz) port
75 g (3 oz) sugar
1 cinnamon stick

To Serve:
clotted cream

1 To make the almond pastry, in a bowl, beat the butter and sugar together until pale and creamy, then gradually beat in the egg, taking care not to curdle the mixture. Stir in the ground almonds and flour to make a soft, smooth dough. Wrap in cling film and leave to rest in the refrigerator for at least 3 hours, or preferably overnight.

2 To make the frangipan, in a bowl, beat the butter with the sugar until light and fluffy, then stir in the flour, ground almonds and egg.

3 To make the sauce, put half of the plums in a pan with the port, sugar, cinnamon stick and sufficient water to just cover. Bring to a simmer and cook gently until the plums are soft. Discard the cinnamon. Purée in a blender or food processor, then pass through a chinois (fine sieve). Check the sweetness, adding more sugar if necessary.

4 Finely slice the remaining plums.

5 Roll out the pastry thinly and use to line four 10 cm (4 inch) individual flan tins. Spread the frangipan over the base of the pastry cases and arrange the plum slices in an overlapping circle on top. Bake in a preheated oven at 180°C (350°F) mark 4 for 30-40 minutes. Transfer to a wire rack to cool.

6 To serve, unmould a tart onto the centre of each serving plate. Drizzle over the plum sauce and add a dollop of clotted cream. Serve warm or cold.

Individual Glazed Baked Lemon Tarts with Lemon Curd Ice Cream

Sweet Pastry:
180 g (6½ oz) unsalted butter, softened
60 g (2¼ oz) caster sugar
pinch of salt
250 g (9 oz) plain flour
1 egg yolk (size 3)
15 ml (1 tbsp) cold water

Lemon Filling:
3 eggs
140 g (4¾ oz) caster sugar
finely grated zest and juice of 1½ lemons
150 ml (¼ pint) double cream

To Finish:
icing sugar, for dusting

Ice Cream:
150 ml (¼ pint) double cream
150 ml (¼ pint) full-fat milk
3 egg yolks
75 g (3 oz) caster sugar
45 ml (3 tbsp) lemon curd (preferably homemade)

1 First make the ice cream. Pour the cream and milk into a saucepan and slowly bring to the boil. Meanwhile, beat the egg yolks and sugar together in a bowl until pale and light. Pour on the hot milk and cream, whisking all the time. Stir in the lemon curd and allow to cool. When the mixture is cold, churn in an ice-cream maker until frozen.

2 To make the pastry, cream the butter, sugar and salt together in a bowl, or using a food processor, until light and fluffy. Add 50 g (2 oz) of the flour and mix until evenly blended, then mix in the remaining flour, egg yolk and water to form a soft dough. Turn out onto a lightly floured surface and knead gently, then wrap in cling film and leave to rest in the refrigerator for at least 1 hour.

3 Roll out the pastry thinly and use to line four 10 cm (4 inch) loose-bottomed flan tins. Chill in the refrigerator for 15 minutes. Line with greaseproof paper and baking beans and bake blind in a preheated oven at 200°C (400°F) mark 6 for 10-12 minutes. Remove the paper and beans and return to the oven for a further 8-10 minutes until cooked. Reduce the oven setting to 170°C (325°F) mark 3.

4 To make the filling, whisk the eggs, sugar, lemon zest and juice together until well blended. Whisk in the cream, cover and refrigerate until needed.

5 Pour the lemon filling into the flan cases and bake in the oven for 25 minutes until just set. Allow to cool.

6 Just before serving, carefully remove the flans from their tins. Dust the tops with icing sugar and glaze with a blow torch or under a preheated hot grill, protecting the pastry edges with strips of foil if necessary.

7 Place each flan on a serving plate and add a scoop of lemon ice cream. Serve at once, dusted with icing sugar.

Tart Lemon Tart with Blackberry Sauce

Pastry:
100 g (4 oz) plain flour
pinch of salt
25 g (1 oz) icing sugar
50 g (2 oz) butter, softened
few drops of almond essence (optional)
1 medium egg yolk
30-45 ml (2-3 tbsp) water
beaten egg white, for brushing

Filling:
4 large eggs
125 g (4 oz) caster sugar
finely grated zest of 3 lemons
190 ml (6½ fl oz) lemon juice
140 ml (4½ fl oz) whipping cream

Blackberry Sauce:
100 g (4 oz) blackberries
25 g (1 oz) icing sugar
10 ml (2 tsp) lemon juice
10 ml (2 tsp) crème de cassis (optional)

To Serve:
45 ml (3 tbsp) mascarpone
45 ml (3 tbsp) crème fraîche
icing sugar, for dusting

1 To make the pastry, place all the ingredients in a food processor and process until a ball of dough is formed; do not over-mix. Turn out and knead gently on a lightly floured surface until smooth. Wrap in cling film and rest in the refrigerator for 30-40 minutes. Preheat a baking sheet in the oven.

2 Roll out the pastry thinly on a lightly floured surface. Use to line a 23 cm (9 inch) loose-based fluted flan tin which is 2.5 cm (1 inch) deep, extending the pastry 3 mm (⅛ inch) above the rim to allow for shrinkage. Prick the base with a fork and brush all over with beaten egg white. Place on the preheated baking sheet and bake in a preheated oven at 200°C (400°F) mark 6 for about 10 minutes until golden. Lower the oven setting to 180°C (350°F) mark 4.

3 To make the filling, lightly whisk the eggs and sugar together in a bowl until evenly mixed; don't over-beat. Add the lemon zest and juice, then the cream and whisk again until smooth.

4 Pour the filling into the pastry case and bake for about 30 minutes or until the filling is set and springy to the touch.

5 Meanwhile to make the sauce, put the blackberries, icing sugar and lemon juice in a food processor and work to a purée. Pass through a sieve into a bowl and add cassis to taste. Taste and add a little more lemon juice if required.

6 To serve, mix the mascarpone with the crème fraîche. Dust the tarts with icing sugar and place on individual plates. Surround with the blackberry sauce and serve with a dollop of the mascarpone crème fraîche mixture.

Pistachio and Honey Rolls with Cinnamon-flavoured Yogurt

Syrup:
125 g (4 oz) granulated sugar
150 ml (¼ pint) water
15 ml (1 tbsp) honey
strip of cassia bark, or 1 cinnamon stick
zest of 1 orange (removed in strips with a zester)
15 ml (1 tbsp) orange-flower water

Rolls:
225 g (8 oz) filo pastry
125 g (4 oz) unsalted butter, melted

Filling:
50 g (2 oz) shelled pistachio nuts, finely chopped
2.5 ml (½ tsp) ground cinnamon
125 g (4 oz) ground almonds
15 ml (1 tbsp) water
50 g (2 oz) brown sugar

Cinnamon Yogurt:
150 ml (¼ pint) Greek-style yogurt
2.5 ml (½ tsp) ground cinnamon
10 ml (2 tsp) orange-flower water

1 First make the syrup. Put the sugar and water into a small heavy-based pan and heat slowly until the sugar is dissolved. Add the honey, cassia bark or cinnamon stick and the orange zest. Bring to the boil and boil hard for 5 minutes, then remove from the heat. Add the orange-flower water and set aside until the syrup is cold.

2 Open out the filo pastry and cut through the layers into three rectangles; this gives 36 slices, each about 30 x 10 cm (12 x 4 inches). Keep covered with a clean tea-towel to prevent the pastry drying out.

3 Put all the filling ingredients in a bowl and mix together with your fingers to form a stiff paste. Shape into 18 small rolls.

4 Taking two strips of pastry at a time, brush well with butter and lay one strip on top of the other. Place a roll of filling at one end, fold over the pastry edges, then roll up to the end. Place in a buttered rectangular baking tin, seam-side down. Continue until all the pastry and filling is used up. Brush the remaining butter over the top of the rolls.

5 Bake in a preheated oven at 180°C (350°F) mark 4 for 20 minutes until the tops are crisp and brown. Carefully separate the rolls and turn them over. Bake for a further 10-15 minutes until browned all over. Immediately pour the cold syrup over the rolls; leave until cold.

6 To prepare the cinnamon yogurt, mix the ground cinnamon with the orange-flower water, then stir in the yogurt until evenly blended. Chill until required.

7 Serve the pistachio and honey rolls accompanied by the flavoured yogurt.

Note: To ensure the pastry remains crisp, it is important that the pastries are hot and the syrup is cold when it is poured over.

Baked Pears with a Caramelised Mead Syrup and Fresh Ginger Ice Cream

4 small ripe but firm pears (preferably Rocha)
250 ml (8 fl oz) mead
3 cinnamon sticks
1 cm (½ inch) piece fresh root ginger, peeled and sliced
175 g (6 oz) sugar

Ginger Ice Cream:
250 ml (8 fl oz) sugar syrup (see below)
45 ml (3 tbsp) chopped fresh root ginger
350 ml (12 fl oz) full-fat milk
3 egg yolks (size 2)
1.25 ml (¼ tsp) vanilla extract
225 g (8 oz) mascarpone cheese

1 First make the ice cream. Put the sugar syrup and ginger in a small heavy-based pan, bring to the boil and simmer, uncovered, for 5 minutes. Meanwhile, bring the milk to just below the boil in another pan. Remove from the heat and pour in the ginger syrup. Cover and leave to infuse for 30 minutes.

2 Lightly beat the egg yolks in a heatproof bowl. Reheat the milk and syrup to just below boiling point, then pour onto the egg yolks in a thin stream, whisking vigorously all the time. Stand the bowl over a pan of simmering water and stir until the custard is thick enough to lightly coat the back of a spoon; do not let it boil. (Alternatively cook the custard in a heavy-based pan set on a heat-diffuser mat.) Immediately plunge the base of the pan into cold water to stop further cooking. Let cool completely, then cover and chill thoroughly.

3 Strain the chilled custard through a fine sieve into a bowl and add the vanilla extract. Stir the mascarpone cheese in a bowl to loosen it, then add the custard in a thin continuous stream, stirring all the time until the mixture is smooth. Transfer to an ice-cream maker and churn for 20 minutes. Turn into a freezerproof container and freeze until required.

4 Peel the pears (using a canelle knife if preferred to remove the skins in strips, leaving a decorative pattern). Halve them lengthwise and scoop out the cores.

5 Place the pears, cut-side down, in an ovenproof dish and pour over the mead. Scatter the cinnamon and ginger into the dish. Cover with foil and bake in a preheated oven at 200°C (400°F) mark 6 for 35-45 minutes until the pears are tender but not soft. Drain the pears, reserving the mead, and set aside to cool. Strain the mead.

6 To make the caramel, put the sugar and half of the mead in a heavy-based pan over a low heat until the sugar is dissolved, then increase the heat and cook steadily until the syrup registers 160°C (320°F) on a sugar thermometer and forms a light caramel. Immediately remove from the heat and allow to cool, occasionally adding a spoonful of mead until you obtain a cool syrup of pouring consistency.

7 To serve, place two pear halves on each serving plate with a scoop of ginger ice cream. Drizzle over some of the caramel syrup and serve at once.

Sugar Syrup: Dissolve 225 g (8 oz) granulated sugar in 250 ml (8 fl oz) water in a heavy-based pan over a low heat, then bring to the boil. Remove from the heat and allow to cool. Use as required.

Roast Pears with Honey Ice Cream

4 large firm, ripe dessert pears
50 g (2 oz) unsalted butter, melted
75 g (3 oz) caster sugar
juice of 1 lemon
120 ml (8 tbsp) crème de cassis

Honey Ice Cream:
6 egg yolks (size 2)
65 g (2½ oz) caster sugar
500 ml (16 fl oz) full-fat milk
150 g (5½ oz) thin honey (preferably lemon blossom)
100 ml (3½ fl oz) double cream

To Serve:
caster sugar, for sprinkling
small mint leaves, to decorate
Shortbread Biscuits (see right)

1 First make the ice cream. Whisk the egg yolks and sugar together in a bowl until pale in colour. Slowly bring the milk to the boil in a heavy-based pan, then gradually add to the egg mixture, whisking all the time. Pour back into the pan and place over a low heat. Stir continually until the custard thickens enough to coat the back of a wooden spoon. Remove from the heat. Allow to cool slightly, then beat in the honey and cream. Let cool completely, then put into an ice-cream maker and churn for 20 minutes until frozen. (If not serving immediately, transfer to a freezer-proof container and place in the freezer.)

2 Peel, quarter and core the pears, reserving peelings. Place pears in an ovenproof dish with 50 g (2 oz) of the sugar, half of the lemon juice and half of the cassis. Bake in the oven at 200°C (400°F) mark 6 for 30-40 minutes or until tender, basting with the cooking juices from time to time.

3 Meanwhile, put the pear peelings in a small pan with just enough water to cover. Add remaining sugar, lemon juice and cassis. Bring to the boil, lower heat and simmer gently until syrupy. Strain into a clean pan.

4 Remove pears from oven and add any residual cooking juices to the pear syrup. Reheat and reduce slightly if necessary.

5 Place the pear quarters on a baking sheet, sprinkle with sugar and caramelise under a hot grill (or use a blow torch). Arrange 4 pear quarters on each serving plate around a scoop of honey ice cream. Decorate with mint and serve with the biscuits.

Shortbread Biscuits

100 g (4 oz) slightly salted butter, softened
50 g (2 oz) caster sugar
125 g (5 oz) plain flour, sifted
25 g (1 oz) fine semolina
finely grated zest of ½ lemon
caster sugar, for sprinkling

1 Cream the butter and sugar together in a bowl until light and fluffy. Stir in the lemon zest. Using a wooden spoon, stir in the flour, followed by the semolina. Gather the dough with your hands and knead lightly until it forms a soft ball.

2 Turn the dough onto a lightly floured surface and roll out to a 5 mm (¼ inch) thickness. Cut out stars or other shapes, using an appropriate pastry cutter.

3 Place on a buttered baking sheet and sprinkle lightly with caster sugar. Bake in a preheated oven at 170°C (325°F) mark 3 for 10-12 minutes until starting to colour. Leave on the baking sheet for 5 minutes, then transfer to a wire rack to cool.

Strawberries with Sablé Biscuits, Orange and Lemon Syllabub and Raspberry Sauce

450 g (1 lb) strawberries, halved if large

Sablé Pastry:
140 g (5 oz) plain flour
pinch of salt
110 g (4 oz) butter, softened
1 egg yolk
55 g (2 oz) icing sugar, sifted
2 drops of vanilla essence

Raspberry Sauce:
225 g (8 oz) raspberries
75 g (3 oz) icing sugar
squeeze of lemon juice, to taste

Syllabub:
50 g (2 oz) caster sugar
75 ml (5 tbsp) sherry
juice and finely grated zest of ½ orange
juice and finely grated zest of ½ lemon
300 ml (½ pint) double cream

To Finish:
icing sugar, for dusting

1 For the raspberry sauce, place the raspberries in a bowl, cover with the icing sugar and leave to macerate for at least 1 hour. Purée the mixture in a blender or food processor, then pass through a fine nylon sieve into a bowl. Add lemon juice to taste.

2 To make the sablé pastry, sift the flour and salt onto a board. Make a large well in the centre and add the butter. Add the egg yolk, icing sugar and vanilla essence to the butter. Using your fingertips 'peck' the butter, egg yolk and sugar together, mixing to a soft paste. Then gradually draw in the flour to make a soft dough. Knead lightly until the pastry is smooth. Wrap in cling film and leave to rest in the refrigerator for at least 30 minutes.

3 When the pastry is firm enough, roll out thinly on a lightly floured surface. Cut out 8 rounds, using a 7.5 cm (3 inch) fluted cutter. Transfer to a baking sheet and cook in a preheated oven at 200°C (400°F) mark 6 for 8 minutes. Using a palette knife, transfer the biscuits to a wire rack and leave to cool.

4 To make the syllabub, combine the sugar, sherry and citrus zests and juices in a bowl. Whip the cream in another bowl until soft peaks form, then add the sherry mixture and beat until the mixture is thick enough to hold its shape.

5 To serve, place a sablé biscuit on each serving plate and spoon the syllabub on top. Cover with the strawberries, reserving a few for decoration. Top with the remaining biscuits. Dust with icing sugar. Roll the reserved strawberries in a little raspberry sauce and place on top of the sablé towers. Pour some raspberry sauce around the biscuits and serve at once.

Turkish Delight Figs

175 g (6 oz) granulated sugar
175 ml (6 fl oz) water
30 ml (2 tbsp) rosewater
30 ml (2 tbsp) orange flower water
juice of 1 lemon
4 large or 8 small fresh figs

To Serve:
Greek-style yogurt
Sum Sum Biscuits (see right)

1 Dissolve the sugar in the water in a small heavy-based saucepan over a low heat. Increase the heat, bring to the boil and boil rapidly for 5 minutes. Add the rosewater, orange flower water and lemon juice. Bring back to the boil and simmer for 2 minutes. Remove from the heat.

2 Carefully cut the figs vertically into quarters, leaving them intact at the base. Arrange on a flat, heatproof dish and spoon the hot syrup over them. Set aside to cool, basting with the syrup occasionally. Serve at room temperature, with yogurt and the biscuits.

Sum Sum Biscuits

120 g (4 oz) butter, softened
60 g (2 oz) caster sugar
150 g (5 oz) plain flour
1 egg white, lightly beaten
15 ml (1 tbsp) granulated sugar
2.5 ml (½ tsp) ground cinnamon
120 g (4 oz) sesame seeds

1 Beat the butter and sugar together in a bowl until very soft and creamy. Gradually work in the flour. Mix well and knead to a slightly sticky mixture.

2 Mix the egg white, granulated sugar, cinnamon and sesame seeds together in a bowl and spread half of this mixture on a flat plate.

3 Take a small amount of the biscuit mixture and roll into a ball, about the size of a walnut. Press down lightly on to the sesame seeds and flatten gently with two fingers to a round biscuit, about 7.5 cm (3 inches) in diameter. Carefully lift with a fish slice and flip over onto a greased baking sheet, sesame side-up. Repeat until all the mixture is used, spacing the biscuits well apart; you will need to use 2 baking sheets. You should make about 16 biscuits.

4 Bake in a preheated oven at 200°C (400°F) mark 6 for 10-15 minutes until golden brown – watch carefully as they quickly burn. Leave to cool on the baking sheets, then carefully remove by sliding a sharp knife underneath. The biscuits will be very crisp.

White Chocolate Torte with Orange Caramel Sauce

Praline:
50 g (2 oz) sugar
10 ml (2 tsp) water
50 g (2 oz) skinned hazelnuts, toasted

Sponge:
1 egg (size 1)
40 g (1½ oz) caster sugar
20 g (¾ oz) self-raising flour
20 g (¾ oz) ground almonds

Mousse Filling:
175 g (6 oz) white chocolate
⅓ sachet powdered gelatine
15 ml (1 tbsp) warm water
1 egg yolk (size 1)
45 ml (3 tbsp) fromage frais
2 egg whites (size 1)
30 ml (2 tbsp) crushed praline (see above)

Orange Caramel Sauce:
75 g (3 oz) granulated sugar
15 ml (1 tbsp) water
juice of 2 oranges
5 ml (1 tsp) cornflour, mixed with 10 ml (2 tsp) water (optional)

To Finish:
icing sugar, for dusting

1 To make the praline, put the sugar and water in a heavy-based pan and dissolve over a low heat. Increase the heat and cook to a nut brown caramel. Carefully add the hazelnuts, then immediately pour into a shallow oiled baking tin. Leave until set hard, then grind to a powder using a food processor or blender; set aside.

2 Grease a 15 cm (6 inch) round cake tin and line with non-stick baking parchment. For the sponge, whisk the egg and caster sugar together in a bowl until the mixture leaves a thick trail when the beaters are lifted. Gently fold in the flour and ground almonds.

3 Pour the mixture into the cake tin and bake in a preheated oven at 180°C (350°F) mark 4 for 20 minutes until the sponge springs back when lightly pressed. Leave in the tin for 5 minutes, then transfer to a wire rack to cool. Clean the cake tin and line with fresh baking parchment.

4 Whilst the sponge is baking, prepare the mousse filling. Melt the chocolate in a heatproof bowl placed over a pan of simmering water. In a small cup, dissolve the gelatine in 15 ml (1 tbsp) warm water. Allow the chocolate to cool a little, then beat in the egg yolk, followed by the fromage frais. Add the dissolved gelatine in a thin stream, stirring all the time.

5 Whisk the egg whites in a separate bowl until they form soft peaks. Fold into the chocolate mixture with the 30 ml (2 tbsp) crushed praline.

6 Split the sponge into two layers and place the bottom half in the cake tin. Pour on the chocolate mousse filling. Chill in the refrigerator for 1 hour or until set, then place the second sponge layer on top.

7 For the orange caramel sauce, put the sugar and 15 ml (1 tbsp) water in a heavy-based saucepan and heat gently until dissolved. Increase the heat and cook to a golden caramel. Carefully, as the mixture may splutter, stir in the orange juice. The sauce should be the consistency of runny honey. If too thin, add the cornflour and cook, stirring, until slightly thickened.

8 To serve, cut the torte into slices, dredge with icing sugar and serve each portion on a pool of orange sauce.

Chocolate Whiskey Cake with Amaretti Crème Fraîche

50 g (2 oz) chopped stoned prunes
30-45 ml (2-3 tbsp) Irish whiskey
75 g (3 oz) good quality plain chocolate,
*   in pieces*
45-60 ml (3-4 tbsp) strong black coffee,
*   cooled*
50 g (2 oz) unsalted butter
40 g (1½ oz) caster sugar
2 eggs (size 2), separated
50 g (2 oz) pecan nuts, chopped
25 g (1 oz) ground almonds
few drops of almond essence
25 g (1 oz) plain flour, sifted

Icing:
75 g (3 oz) good-quality plain chocolate
22 ml (1½ tbsp) whiskey
75 g (3 oz) unsalted butter

Amaretti Crème Fraîche:
90 ml (6 tbsp) crème fraîche
8 amaretti biscuits, crushed
1-2 drops almond essence
5 ml (1 tsp) amaretto liqueur, or to taste

To Finish:
icing sugar, for dusting

1 Soak the prunes in the whiskey for several hours, or overnight if possible.

2 Butter and flour four 10 cm (4 inch) individual cake tins (see note).

3 Melt the chocolate with the coffee in a heatproof bowl over a pan of simmering water. Allow to cool.

4 In another bowl, cream the butter with all but 7.5 ml (½ tbsp) of the sugar until light and fluffy. Beat in the egg yolks, a little at a time.

5 In a separate bowl, whisk the egg whites until stiff, then gradually whisk in the remaining sugar.

6 Stir the melted chocolate into the creamed mixture until evenly blended, then stir in the pecan nuts and prunes together with any remaining soaking liquor. Fold in the ground almonds and almond essence. Fold in the whisked egg whites alternately with the flour (a quarter at a time).

7 Divide the mixture between the prepared tins and bake in the centre of a preheated oven at 180°C (350°F) mark 4 for 15-20 minutes, or until a skewer inserted into the centre of the cakes comes out clean. Turn out onto a wire rack and allow to cool before icing.

8 To make the icing, melt the chocolate with the whiskey in a bowl over a pan of simmering water. Stir until smooth, then remove from the heat and beat in the butter a little at a time. Stand the bowl over a bowl or pan of cold water to cool the icing until it reaches a spreading consistency.

9 To make the amaretti crème fraîche, stir all the ingredients together in a bowl until evenly blended. Cover and chill in the refrigerator until required.

10 When the icing has reached the correct consistency, spread over the top and sides of the cakes and smooth with a warm palette knife. Serve on individual plates, dusted with icing sugar and accompanied by the amaretti crème fraîche.

Note: If you do not have individual cake tins, use Yorkshire pudding tins instead.

Chocolate, Almond and Hazelnut Torte with Mascarpone Ice Cream

110 g (4 oz) blanched whole almonds
110 g (4 oz) roasted hazelnuts
225 g (8 oz) fine quality bitter chocolate
 (70% cocoa butter)
225 g (8 oz) unsalted butter
225 g (8 oz) caster sugar
4 eggs (size 1), separated

Mascarpone Ice Cream:
40 g (1½ oz) caster sugar
30 ml (1 fl oz) water
juice of ½ lemon
2 egg yolks (size 2)
225 g (8 oz) mascarpone cheese
45 ml (3 tbsp) Greek-style yogurt

1 First make the ice cream. Put the sugar, water and lemon juice in a saucepan and dissolve over a low heat, then bring to the boil and simmer for 1-2 minutes to form a syrup.

2 Beat the egg yolks in a heatproof bowl until pale, then slowly add the hot syrup, whisking continuously. Stand the bowl over a pan of simmering water (making sure that the water does not come into contact with the bowl) and continue to whisk for approximately 7 minutes, until the mixture becomes thick and creamy.

3 Remove the bowl from the heat and whisk until the mixture is cool.

4 Whisk in the mascarpone, then stir in yogurt. Transfer the mixture to an ice-cream machine and churn until frozen.

5 For the torte, butter and line a deep 20 cm (8 inch) loose-bottomed cake tin with greaseproof paper. Grind the almonds, hazelnuts and chocolate fairly coarsely, using a food processor.

6 Cream the butter and sugar together in a mixing bowl until light and fluffy. Beat in the egg yolks, then fold in the chocolate and nuts.

7 In a separate bowl, whisk the egg whites until they form soft peaks. Gently fold the egg whites into the chocolate and nut mixture. Pour into the cake tin.

8 Bake in a preheated oven at 150°C (300°F) mark 2 for about 50 minutes, until set. A skewer inserted into the middle of the torte should come out clean if the torte is cooked. Leave in the tin for about 5 minutes, then carefully transfer to a wire rack and leave to cool.

9 Serve the torte cut into wedges, accompanied by the mascarpone ice cream.

Trio of Chocolate, Pistachio and Vanilla Crème Brûlée

900 ml (1½ pints) double cream
1 vanilla pod, split
12 egg yolks
125 g (4 oz) caster sugar
50 g (2 oz) good quality plain chocolate (Valrhona), finely chopped
25 g (1 oz) pistachio paste

To Finish:
50 g (2 oz) caster sugar

1 Pour the cream into a heavy-based saucepan, add the vanilla pod with its seeds and slowly bring to the boil. Remove from the heat and leave to infuse for about 10 minutes.

2 Meanwhile, whisk the egg yolks and sugar together in a bowl until smooth, light and creamy. Pour on the hot cream, whisking all the time.

3 Return the mixture to the pan and cook over a low heat, stirring constantly, until thickened enough to coat the back of the wooden spoon.

4 Strain the mixture through a fine sieve and divide into 3 equal portions. Add the chopped chocolate to one portion, stirring until melted. Add the pistachio paste to the second portion and stir until evenly blended. The third portion is the vanilla crème.

5 Stand 12 small ramekins on a tray. Fill four ramekins with the chocolate crème, four with the pistachio crème and four with the vanilla crème. Let cool, then chill in the refrigerator for 2 hours or until set.

6 To finish, sprinkle an even layer of sugar on top of each crème and caramelise under a preheated hot grill. (Alternatively, use a blow torch.)

7 To serve, place one ramekin of each flavoured crème brûlée on each serving plate to form a trio.

Rhubarb Creme Brulée

2 egg yolks
40 g (1½ oz) caster sugar
60 ml (2 fl oz) milk
160 ml (5½ fl oz) double cream
2 vanilla pods, split
150 g (5 oz) rhubarb, trimmed
70 g (2½ oz) granulated sugar
200 ml (7 fl oz) water
60 ml (4 tbsp) demerara sugar

1 Beat the egg yolks and caster sugar together in a bowl.

2 Put the milk, double cream and vanilla pods in a saucepan and bring slowly to the boil. Pour onto the egg mixture, whisking all the time.

3 Cut the rhubarb into 1 cm (½ inch) pieces.

4 Dissolve the granulated sugar in the water in a saucepan over a low heat to make a syrup.

5 Add the rhubarb to the syrup and poach for 2 minutes only. Drain thoroughly.

6 Divide the rhubarb between 4 ramekins. Strain the cream mixture and pour into the ramekins.

7 Stand the ramekins in a bain-marie (or roasting tin containing enough hot water to come halfway up the sides of the dishes). Cook in a preheated oven at 150°C (300°F) mark 2 for 45-55 minutes or until set. Take the ramekins out of the bain-marie and allow to cool.

8 Sprinkle the demerara sugar over the surface of each crème brulée and place under a hot grill for 2-3 minutes until the sugar is caramelised. (Alternatively, use a blow-torch.) Chill until ready to serve.

Dark Chocolate Teardrops filled with a White Chocolate Mousse and an Apricot Compote, served with a Bitter Orange Sauce

To shape the chocolate teardrops, you will need a few A4 sheets of acetate (clear plastic) and paperclips or small bulldog clips.

Dark Chocolate Teardrops:
225 g (8 oz) plain dark chocolate

White Chocolate Mousse:
3 egg yolks
40 g (1½ oz) caster sugar
25 g (1 oz) plain flour
200 ml (7 fl oz) milk
200 g (7 oz) white chocolate
300 ml (½ pint) double cream

Apricot Compote:
225 g (8 oz) dried apricots
250 ml (8 fl oz) freshly squeezed orange juice
finely grated zest and juice of 1 lemon

Orange Sauce:
175 ml (6 fl oz) frozen concentrated orange juice, thawed
50 g (2 oz) sugar
30 ml (2 tbsp) Grand Marnier
2.5 ml (½ tsp) arrowroot
2.5 ml (½ tsp) water

To Decorate:
8 orange slices
40 ml (8 tsp) demerara sugar

1 To make the chocolate teardrops, melt the dark chocolate in a heatproof bowl over a pan of simmering water. Meanwhile, cut at least 4 strips of acetate approximately 23 x 5 cm (9 x 2 inches). Holding the acetate by the corners and curving the strip slightly, dip the outside into the melted chocolate, moving it from side to side to coat one side of the acetate strip with chocolate, shaking off excess. Curve the strip slightly the other way so that the chocolate is on the inside and clip two corners at one end of the strip together to form a teardrop shape. Lay on a tray lined with greaseproof paper and chill in the refrigerator until set.

2 To prepare the mousse, beat the egg yolks and sugar together in a bowl until pale and creamy. Add the flour and whisk until smooth. Bring the milk to the boil in a heavy-based pan. Gradually add to the mixture, whisking all the time. Return to the pan and stir over a low heat until thickened; take off the heat. Meanwhile, melt the white chocolate in a bowl over a pan of simmering water. Stir into the custard mixture and leave to cool. When cold, whip the cream until soft peaks form and fold into the mousse. Chill in the refrigerator while making the compote.

3 For the compote, put the apricots, orange juice, lemon zest and juice into a pan and cook gently for about 10 minutes until most of the liquid has evaporated and the apricots are tender. Purée in a blender or food processor, then transfer to a bowl and set aside to cool.

4 With the acetate still in position, half-fill the chocolate teardrops with the white chocolate mousse. Cover with a layer of apricot compote, then fill the teardrops to the top with mousse. Smooth with a palette knife and return to the refrigerator to chill for 1½ to 2 hours.

5 To make the orange sauce, put the orange juice, sugar and Grand Marnier in a saucepan and slowly bring to the boil, stirring until the sugar is dissolved. Let bubble to reduce by one third. Meanwhile, mix the arrowroot with the cold water. Stir into the orange sauce and cook, stirring, until thickened. Set aside to cool.

6 For the decoration, sprinkle the orange slices with demerara sugar and caramelise under a preheated hot grill (or using a blowtorch).

7 To serve, position a teardrop on one side of each serving plate, carefully peeling away the plastic strip; cut the non-pointed end of the teardrop with scissors to give a clean edge. Pipe a thin ring of melted chocolate onto each plate, to form a well for the sauce; spoon in the orange sauce. Decorate with the caramelised orange slices and serve at once.

Orange and Grand Marnier Soufflé in Meringue, served on a Chocolate Sauce

Chocolate Discs:
50 g (2 oz) good quality plain dark chocolate

Meringues:
2 egg whites
110 g (4 oz) caster sugar

Chocolate Sauce:
50 g (2 oz) good quality dark chocolate
knob of unsalted butter
60 ml (2 fl oz) whipping cream
15 g (½ oz) caster sugar

Soufflé:
1 sachet powdered gelatine
juice of ½ lemon
30 ml (2 tbsp) water
3 egg yolks
125 g (4 oz) caster sugar
150 ml (¼ pint) orange juice
150 ml (¼ pint) whipping cream
10 ml (2 tsp) Grand Marnier
2 egg whites

To Finish:
60 ml (4 tbsp) whipped cream
few chopped pistachio nuts
few orange segments
few raspberries
mint sprigs, to decorate

1 To make the chocolate discs, melt the chocolate in a heatproof bowl over a pan of hot water. Meanwhile, draw 4 oblongs, each about 7.5 x 5 cm (3 x 2 inches), on a sheet of baking parchment, placed on a board. Fill the oblongs with the chocolate, spreading it evenly and leave in a cool place until set.

2 To make the meringues, whisk the egg whites in a bowl until firm but not dry. Gradually whisk in the caster sugar, a spoonful at a time.

3 Draw 12 oblongs (the same size as the chocolate discs) on a large baking sheet lined with non-stick baking parchment. Using a piping bag fitted with a 1 cm (½ inch) plain or fluted nozzle pipe along the lines joining the ends to form 12 oblong 'rings'. Bake in a preheated oven at 120°C (240°F) mark ¼-½ for 40-50 minutes until firm and crisp. Cool on a wire rack.

4 To make the chocolate sauce, melt the chocolate with the butter in a heatproof bowl over a pan of hot water. Stir until smooth, remove from the heat and let cool slightly, then stir in the cream and sugar.

5 To prepare the soufflé, sprinkle the gelatine over the lemon juice and water in a small heatproof bowl and leave to soak for 2-3 minutes. Stand the bowl over a pan of simmering water until the gelatine is dissolved.

6 Meanwhile, whisk the egg yolks and sugar together in a bowl until thick and mousse-like. Add the gelatine mixture to the orange juice, then stir this into the egg yolk mixture.

7 In another bowl, whip the cream with the liqueur until soft peaks form, then fold into the mousse. In a clean bowl, whisk the egg whites until they form peaks and fold

into the mousse. Cover and chill in the refrigerator until just set.

8 To assemble, place a chocolate oblong in the centre of each serving plate and carefully pile 3 meringue rings on top to form a 'basket'. Spoon the orange soufflé into the baskets and top with a little whipped cream and a sprinkling of chopped pistachio nuts. Pour the chocolate sauce to one side and decorate with orange segments, raspberries and mint sprigs.

Hazelnut Shortbread with Raspberry Pernod Coulis and White Chocolate Sauce

Shortbread:
110 g (4 oz) extra-fine plain flour
80 g (3 oz) butter, in pieces
40 g (1½ oz) hazelnuts, finely ground
40 g (1½ oz) caster sugar

Raspberry Coulis:
110 g (4 oz) raspberries
30 ml (2 tbsp) Pernod
30 ml (2 tbsp) dark brown sugar

Filling:
70 ml (5 tbsp) whipping cream
5 ml (1 tsp) caster sugar
50 g (2 oz) fromage frais

Chocolate Sauce:
100 g (3½ oz) white chocolate, in pieces
140 ml (¼ pint) single cream

To Assemble:
110 g (4 oz) raspberries
icing sugar, for dusting

1 To make the shortbread, place the flour in a bowl and rub in the butter until the mixture resembles fine breadcrumbs. Add the ground hazelnuts and sugar and work together with your fingertips until the mixture forms a firm dough. Wrap in cling film and leave to rest in the refrigerator for 30 minutes.

2 Meanwhile, put the raspberries, Pernod and brown sugar in a food processor or blender and work to a purée, then pass through a nylon sieve to remove the pips.

3 Roll out the shortbread dough to a 5 mm (¼ inch) thickness and cut out 12 triangles. Transfer to a baking sheet and bake in a preheated oven at 200°C (400°F) mark 6 for 10-12 minutes. Trim the shapes to neaten as soon as you take them out of the oven (using the same cutter).

4 To make the filling, in a bowl whip the cream with the caster sugar, then fold in the fromage frais. Place in a piping bag and keep in the refrigerator until required.

5 To make the chocolate sauce, melt the chocolate in a heatproof bowl over a pan of boiling water. Whisk in the single cream and remove from the heat.

6 To assemble, pipe the fromage frais mixture onto the centre of 8 shortbreads and arrange raspberries around the edge. Carefully assemble in pairs, then position the remaining plain shortbreads on top to make 4 shortbread towers. Dust with icing sugar.

7 To serve, pool a little raspberry coulis onto each serving plate, spoon some white chocolate sauce next to this and place the shortbread tower to one side. Scatter a few raspberries in the chocolate sauce. Dot some white chocolate sauce into the coulis and feather with a skewer to decorate.

Bramble and Port Jelly with Lemon Cream

500 g (1 lb 2 oz) blackberries
100 g (3½ oz) sugar
15-30 ml (1-2 tbsp) water
1 cinnamon stick, broken in half
2 gelatine leaves, soaked in a little cold
    water
150 ml (¼ pint) ruby port

Lemon Cream:
300 ml (½ pint) double cream
50 g (2 oz) caster sugar
grated zest and juice of 1 lemon

To Decorate:
finely pared zest of 1 lemon, cut into
    julienne

To Serve:
Langues de Chat (see right)

1 To make the jelly, put the blackberries and sugar in a heavy-based pan with a little water to prevent sticking and cook gently for about 10 minutes until softened. Press through a sieve into a clean bowl.

2 Measure 300 ml (½ pint) blackberry juice for the jelly and pour into the cleaned pan. Add the cinnamon and bring to simmering point.

3 Meanwhile, squeeze the gelatine leaves to remove excess water. Remove the pan from the heat, add the gelatine and whisk until dissolved. Strain into a bowl and leave until on the point of setting.

4 Stir the port into the jelly. Pour into glasses and chill in the refrigerator until set.

5 Meanwhile, to make the lemon cream, whip the cream in a bowl, gradually adding the sugar, lemon zest and juice.

6 For the decoration, blanch the lemon zest julienne in boiling water for 3 minutes; drain thoroughly.

7 To serve, spoon the lemon cream on top of the bramble jelly and decorate with the lemon zest. Serve with the biscuits.

Langues de Chat

3 eggs (size 3)
90 g (3 oz) caster sugar
90 g (3 oz) plain flour
few drops of vanilla essence

1 Whisk the eggs and sugar together in a bowl until pale and thick. Gently fold in the flour and vanilla essence, using a large metal spoon.

2 Put the mixture into a piping bag fitted with a 1 cm (½ inch) plain nozzle and pipe 5 cm (2 inch) lengths on a baking sheet lined with non-stick baking parchment.

3 Bake in a preheated oven at 200°C (400°F) mark 6 for about 7 minutes until pale golden. Leave on the baking sheet for a few minutes to cool slightly, then transfer to a wire rack to cool.

Passion Fruit Chiffon on a Biscuit Base with Mango and Strawberry Coulis

Bases:
50 g (2 oz) 'Rich Tea' biscuits, crushed
25 g (1 oz) caster sugar
15 g (½ oz) flaked almonds
40 g (1½ oz) unsalted butter, melted

Chiffon:
8 passion fruit
2 eggs, separated
110 g (4 oz) caster sugar
15 ml (1 tbsp) lemon or orange juice
7.5 ml (1½ tsp) powdered gelatine
125 ml (4 fl oz) double cream

Mango Coulis:
1 mango
about 60 ml (2 fl oz) sugar syrup (see below)
squeeze of lemon or orange juice (optional)

Strawberry Coulis:
175 g (6 oz) strawberries
about 6 ml (2 fl oz) sugar syrup (see below)
10 ml (2 tsp) lemon juice

1 Mix the crushed biscuits with the sugar and almonds. Add the melted butter and mix well. Press into the base of 4 greased 7.5-10 cm (3-4 inch) loose-bottomed fluted flan tins, which are about 3 cm (1¼ inches) deep.

2 To make the chiffon, halve the passion fruit and scoop out the seeds and pulp into a nylon sieve over a heatproof bowl. Press to extract as much juice as possible. Add the egg yolks and sugar to the strained passion fruit juice and beat well. Place the bowl over a pan of simmering water and continue to beat until the mixture is slightly thickened.

3 Meanwhile, put the lemon or orange juice into a cup, sprinkle on the gelatine and leave to soften, then stand the cup in hot water to dissolve the gelatine.

4 Once the passion fruit mixture is thickened, remove the bowl from the pan and add the dissolved gelatine, stirring well.

5 In a separate bowl, whisk the egg white until it forms soft peaks.

6 In another bowl, whisk the cream until thick.

7 Fold the whipped cream into the passion fruit mixture, then fold in the egg white. Pour the mixture on top of the biscuit bases. Chill in the refrigerator for 2½-3 hours or until set.

8 For the mango coulis, peel the mango and cut 8 thin slices; set aside for the decoration. Cut the rest of the mango flesh away from the stone, chop roughly, then purée in a food processor or blender until smooth. Transfer to a bowl and add sufficient sugar syrup to obtain a sauce consistency.

9 For the strawberry coulis, set aside a few strawberries for decoration. Purée the rest in a blender or food processor, then pass through a fine nylon sieve into a bowl to remove the pips. Add the sugar syrup and lemon juice.

10 To serve, carefully remove the desserts from the flan tins and place on individual serving plates. Surround with the mango and strawberry coulis. Decorate with the reserved fruit and serve at once.

Sugar Syrup: Dissolve 400 g (14 oz) sugar in 300 ml (½ pint) water in a heavy-based pan over a low heat, then bring to the boil and boil for 1-2 minutes to form a syrup. Allow to cool, then use as required.

Grand Marnier Bavarois with Candied Clementines and Caramel Sauce

Bavarois:
225 g (8 oz) caster sugar
40 ml (3 tbsp) water
15 g (½ oz) liquid glucose (optional)
3 egg whites
300 ml (½ pint) milk
5 egg yolks
3 gelatine leaves, soaked in cold water
150 ml (¼ pint) whipping cream
60 ml (4 tbsp) Grand Marnier

Candied Clementines:
6 clementines
100 g (3½ oz) caster sugar
15 ml (1 tbsp) double cream

To Decorate:
3 cubes crystallized ginger, cut into wafer-
   thin slices
spun sugar shapes (optional – see below)

1 To prepare the bavarois, put 175 g (6 oz) of the sugar in a heavy-based pan with the water and glucose if using. Dissolve over a moderate heat, brushing down the sides of the pan with a pastry brush dipped in water. Increase the heat and cook until the syrup registers 120°C (248°F) on a sugar thermometer (ie hard ball stage). In the meantime, beat the egg whites in a bowl until stiff. Pour the hot sugar syrup onto the egg whites (not directly onto the beaters) in a thin stream, beating constantly. Continue to beat at a low speed for about 15 minutes until cool and very stiff; set aside this Italian meringue.

2 Put the milk and half of the remaining sugar in a saucepan and bring to the boil. In a separate bowl, whisk the egg yolks and remaining sugar together until pale and thick enough to leave a ribbon trail when the beaters are lifted. Pour the milk mixture onto the egg yolks, whisking continuously, then return to the pan. Cook, stirring, over a low heat until thickened enough to coat the back of the wooden spoon; do not allow to boil. Squeeze the gelatine leaves to remove excess moisture. Remove the custard from the heat and add the gelatine, stirring until melted. Leave to cool slightly, then strain into a clean bowl.

3 Whip the cream in another bowl until stiff, then stir in the Grand Marnier. Add the Italian meringue to the custard mixture, then fold into the whipped cream. Pour the bavarois mixture into individual moulds and chill until set.

4 Meanwhile, prepare the clementines and sauce. Cut 2 neat crosswise slices from the middle of each clementine. Press the rest of the fruit through a sieve to extract as much juice as possible. Put the sugar in a saucepan and heat gently until melted. Add the clementine slices and heat until the syrup forms a golden caramel. Carefully remove the clementine slices and set aside. Gradually stir the cream into the caramel. Warm the clementine juice and slowly add to the caramel too; allow the sauce to cool.

5 To assemble, carefully unmould a bavarois onto each serving plate. Surround with the caramel sauce and candied clementine slices. Scatter the ginger shavings on top of the bavarois and decorate with spun sugar shapes if desired. Serve at once.

Spun Sugar Shapes: Dissolve 200 g (7 oz) caster sugar in 80 ml (5 tbsp) water with 60 g (2½ oz) liquid glucose in a heavy-based pan over a low heat. Increase the heat and bring to the boil. Cook until the syrup registers 155°C (310°F) brushing down the sides of the pan with a damp pastry brush. Remove from the heat and add 1 - 2 drops of orange colouring. Leave to cool for 3 minutes. Dip a fork into the sugar syrup and drizzle back and forth onto a baking sheet lined with bake-o-glide to form patterns. Allow to cool and harden.

Tangy Lemon Mousse on a Lime Crème in Tuile Baskets with Fruits

3½ gelatine leaves
250 ml (8 fl oz) milk
1 vanilla pod
3 lemons
4 egg yolks
70 g (2¾ oz) caster sugar
250 ml (8 fl oz) whipping cream
4 egg whites

Lime Crème:
175 g (6 fl oz) milk
2 limes
½ vanilla pod
2 egg yolks
15 g (½ oz) caster sugar

To Serve:
1 apple, peeled, cored and thickly sliced
1 orange, peeled and segmented
caster sugar, for coating
4 Tuile Baskets (see overleaf)

1 Soften the gelatine leaves in a shallow dish of cold water.

2 Meanwhile put the milk in a heavy-based pan with the vanilla pod and pared

zest of 1 lemon. Slowly bring to the boil and simmer gently for 5 minutes to infuse. Remove from the heat and allow to cool slightly, then strain.

3 In a bowl, cream together the egg yolks and 50 g (2 oz) of the sugar, until pale. Gradually whisk in the milk, then return to the pan.

4 Cook gently, stirring all the time, until the custard is thick enough to coat the back of the wooden spoon. Remove from the heat. Squeeze the gelatine leaves to remove excess water, then add to the hot custard, stirring to dissolve.

5 Pour into a bowl, stir for 1-2 minutes to cool slightly, then add the grated zest from 2 lemons and the juice from 2½ lemons. Leave to cool for 10 minutes.

6 Lightly whip the cream in another bowl and place in the refrigerator. In another bowl, whisk the egg whites until soft peaks form, then add the remaining 20 g (¾ oz) sugar and juice from the remaining ½ lemon. Whisk until stiff, then fold into the whipped cream. Stir a quarter of this mixture into the lemon gelatine mixture to lighten it, then fold in the remainder. Transfer to a bowl, cover and chill for 2 hours or until set.

7 Meanwhile, prepare the lime crème. Put the milk in a heavy-based saucepan with the pared zest of 1 lime and the ½ vanilla pod. Slowly bring to the boil and simmer gently for 5 minutes to infuse. Let cool slightly, then strain. In a bowl, cream together the egg yolks and sugar. Gradually whisk in the strained milk, then return to the pan. Cook gently, stirring constantly until thick enough to coat the back of the spoon. Turn into a bowl and add the grated zest of 1 lime and the juice from both limes. Allow to cool, then chill.

8 Dip the fruit segments into sugar to coat, then grill under a medium heat, turning occasionally, until golden brown; let cool.

9 To assemble, place a tuile basket on each serving plate and surround with a pool of lime crème. Spoon the lemon mousse into the tuile baskets and decorate with the fruit segments. Serve at once.

Tuile Baskets

125 g (4½ oz) unsalted butter
150 g (5 oz) icing sugar
3 egg whites
125 g (4½ oz) plain flour, sifted
grated zest of 1 lemon

1 Cream the butter and icing sugar together in a bowl until almost white in colour. Stir in the egg white, then fold in the flour and lemon zest. Chill in the refrigerator for 15 minutes.

2 Spread the tuile mixture into 4 rounds, each 10-12 cm (4-5 inches) in diameter, on baking sheets lined with non-stick baking parchment (two to each sheet).

3 Cook, one baking sheet at a time, in a preheated oven at 180°C (350°F) mark 4 for 5-6 minutes. Whilst still warm, carefully transfer each round to the base of an upturned tumbler and shape to form a basket. Leave until firm, then carefully remove. Repeat with the other 2 rounds to make 4 baskets in total.

Chocolate and Ginger Ice Cream Pyramids with an Orange and Passion Fruit Sauce

Nougatine:
60 ml (2 fl oz) water
175 g (6 oz) caster sugar
15 ml (1 tbsp) liquid glucose
30 g (1¼ oz) flaked almonds

Ice Cream:
1 egg
2 egg yolks
50 g (2 oz) muscovado sugar
375 ml (13 fl oz) milk
2 pieces preserved stem ginger in syrup, finely chopped
40 ml (2½ tbsp) ginger syrup (from the jar)
100 ml (3½ fl oz) double cream, whipped
110 g (4 oz) good quality bitter chocolate

Sauce:
4 passion fruit
10 ml (2 tsp) caster sugar
15 ml (1 tbsp) orange juice
5 ml (1 tsp) water
30 ml (2 tbsp) stock syrup (see right)

To Decorate:
1 orange
30 ml (2 tbsp) stock syrup (see right)
20 small mint sprigs

1 To prepare the nougatine, put the water, caster sugar and glucose syrup in a heavy-based pan over a low heat until the sugar is dissolved. Increase the heat and boil, without stirring, to a medium caramel. Remove from the heat, carefully stir in the almonds and immediately pour the mixture onto a lightly oiled baking tray. Allow to cool and set hard.

2 Break up the praline and grind to a powder in a food processor. Spread the powder on a tray to form a square, 3 mm (⅛ inch) thick. Place in a preheated oven at 180°C (350°F) mark 4 for 5 minutes to melt the nougatine. Remove from the oven and allow to cool slightly, then carefully cut into 12 equilateral triangles (see note), using a heavy knife, returning the nougatine to the oven if it becomes too brittle to cut. Store the triangles in an airtight container until needed.

3 To make the ice cream, beat the egg, egg yolks and muscovado sugar together in a bowl. Heat the milk in a heavy-based pan until almost boiling, then pour onto the egg mixture, whisking constantly. Return to the pan and cook over a low heat, whisking all the time, until the custard is thick enough to coat the back of a wooden spoon. Strain into a chilled bowl, allow to cool, then add the stem ginger and syrup. Fold in the whipped cream. Melt the chocolate in a heatproof bowl over a pan of hot water. Let cool slightly, then stir into the custard.

4 Transfer to an ice-cream maker and churn until almost firm. Line 4 pyramid moulds (see note) with cling film and spoon in the ice cream. Place in the freezer until firm.

5 For the sauce, halve the passion fruit and scoop out the flesh and seeds into a small pan. Add the caster sugar, orange juice and 5 ml (1 tsp) water. Bring to a simmer and simmer gently for 2 minutes. Let cool slightly, then whizz in a blender or food processor. Strain through a nylon sieve into a bowl. Add 30 ml (2 tbsp) stock syrup and set aside.

6 For the decoration, finely pare the zest from the orange and cut into julienne. Blanch in boiling water for 15 seconds, refresh in cold water, then repeat this process. Put the blanched julienne into a small pan with the 30 ml (2 tbsp) stock syrup. Bring to the boil, then set aside to cool. Peel and segment the orange, discarding all white pith.

7 To serve, unmould each ice cream pyramid onto the centre of a serving plate and press a nougatine triangle onto each side. Surround with the sauce and decorate with orange segments, orange zest julienne and sprigs of mint.

Stock Syrup: Put 225 g (8 oz) caster sugar and 300 ml (½ pint) water in a pan and dissolve over a low heat. Bring to the boil and boil for 1 minute. Store in a screw-topped jar and use as required.

Note: Pyramid moulds are available from specialist kitchen shops. The ones used for this recipe should measure approximately 7 cm (2¾ inches) along each edge. You need to cut the nougatine triangles a little larger than this, so that they will cover the sides of the ice cream pyramids and enclose them completely.

Rum Punch Parfait with a Medley of Tropical Fruit and Passion Fruit Sauce

Rum Sugar Syrup:
175 g (6 oz) caster sugar
150 ml (¼ pint) water
60 ml (4 tbsp) dark rum

Parfait:
4 egg yolks
120 ml (4 fl oz) rum sugar syrup (see above)
250 ml (8 fl oz) double cream, chilled
30 ml (2 tbsp) rum
2.5 ml (½ tsp) vanilla extract
2.5 ml (½ tsp) angostura bitters
grated zest of ½ lime
15 ml (1 tbsp) lime juice
pinch of freshly grated nutmeg

Passion Fruit Sauce:
5 passion fruit, halved
100 g (4 oz) caster sugar
150 ml (¼ pint) water
5 ml (1 tsp) lime juice
5 ml (1 tsp) lemon juice

Tropical Fruit Medley:
¼ large pineapple, peeled, cored and cut into chunks
1 large mango, peeled, stoned and cubed
1 banana, peeled and sliced
1 large papaya, peeled, deseeded and sliced
8 lychees (fresh or canned)
1 star fruit, sliced
1 kiwi fruit, peeled and sliced

To Serve:
Lemon Clove Stars (see right)

1 To make the sugar syrup, put the sugar, water and rum into a heavy-based saucepan over a low heat until the sugar is dissolved. Increase the heat and bring to the boil. Without stirring, boil until the syrup registers 115°C (239°F) on a sugar thermometer; ie the soft-ball stage.

2 Meanwhile, for the parfait, beat the egg yolks in a bowl until pale. Then slowly pour in 120 ml (4 fl oz) of the hot sugar syrup in a thin stream, whisking all the time. (Do not pour the syrup onto the beaters or it will set!)

3 Continue to beat at maximum speed for 5-10 minutes until the mixture is cool, pale and thickened to a mousse-like mixture. Chill over a bowl of iced water.

4 Whip the chilled cream in a bowl until it forms soft peaks. Gradually fold in the mousse mixture, rum and vanilla extract. Finally add the angostura bitters, lime zest and juice, and the nutmeg. (Note that the flavours will mellow once the mixture is frozen.)

5 Pour the mixture into 6 oiled ramekins and cover each with a disc of greaseproof paper. Freeze until firm.

6 To make the passion fruit sauce, scoop out the seeds from one of the passion fruit and set aside for the decoration. Scoop out the pulp and seeds from the rest, reserving the shells. Dissolve the sugar in the water in a heavy-based pan over a low heat, then bring to the boil and simmer gently until the syrup is clear. Add the passion fruit pulp and seeds, together with the shells. Bring to the boil and simmer for 10 minutes, mashing the shells down into the syrup from time to time. Pass through a sieve and return the sauce to the pan. Simmer to reduce until you have approximately 175 ml (6 fl oz) pink passion fruit juice. Stir in the lemon and lime juices. Allow to cool.

7 Prepare the fruit for the tropical fruit medley, retaining as much juice as possible. Chill until required.

8 About 10 minutes before serving, transfer the parfaits to the refrigerator to soften slightly. Arrange the tropical fruit around the edge of the serving plates and pour over the juices. Unmould a parfait onto the centre of each plate and pour on the passion fruit sauce. Decorate with the reserved passion fruit seeds and serve at once, with the lemon biscuits.

Note: This dessert serves 6.

Lemon Clove Stars

150 g (5 oz) plain flour
pinch of salt
2.5 ml (½ tsp) baking powder
2.5 ml (½ tsp) ground cloves
110 g (4 oz) unsalted butter
75 g (3 oz) light brown sugar
5 ml (1 tsp) vanilla essence
15 ml (1 tbsp) finely grated lemon zest
few drops of lemon oil
icing sugar, for dusting

1 Sift the flour, salt, baking powder and cloves together.

2 Using an electric mixer, cream the butter and sugar together until light and well blended. Add the vanilla essence, then beat in the flour, a quarter at a time. Finally add the lemon zest and oil, beating until the dough forms a ball. If the mixture appears too dry, mix in a few drops of water.

3 Roll out the biscuit dough thinly and cut out stars, using a suitable cutter. Using a palette knife, lift them onto a baking sheet lined with non-stick baking parchment and chill in the refrigerator for 30 minutes.

4 Cook the biscuits in a preheated oven at 180°C (350°F) mark 4 for 8-10 minutes until pale golden brown. Leave on the baking sheet for a few minutes to firm up, then transfer to a wire rack to cool. Serve dusted with icing sugar.

Passion Fruit Sorbet in a Meringue Basket served with a Gratin of Summer Fruits and a Bailey's Sabayon

Meringue:
2 egg whites
50 g (2 oz) caster sugar
50 g (2 oz) icing sugar

Sorbet:
12 passion fruit
300 ml (½ pint) stock syrup (see below)
squeeze of lemon juice

Sabayon:
2 egg yolks
50 g (2 oz) caster sugar
120 ml (4 fl oz) double cream
60 ml (2 fl oz) Bailey's Irish cream

To Serve:
selection of summer fruits (strawberries, raspberries, blackberries, blackcurrants, redcurrants)
mint sprigs, to decorate

1 To make the meringue, whisk the egg whites in a bowl until soft peaks form, then gradually beat in the caster sugar a little at a time. Continue to whisk for a further 10 minutes until stiff and shiny. Gradually sift in the icing sugar and fold in gently, using a slotted spoon.

2 Draw four 5 cm (2 inch) circles on a baking sheet lined with non-stick baking parchment and invert the paper. Using a piping bag fitted with a plain nozzle, pipe a spiral of meringue to cover each circle, to make 4 meringue bases. Pipe an extra ring on the outer edge to form baskets. Using a star nozzle, pipe 5 decorative stars around the edge of each basket. For the basket lids, use an upturned bun tin. Grease 4 of the 'domes' thoroughly and, using a very small plain nozzle, pipe a lacy pattern similar to a spider's web all over – this will form a lid.

3 Cook all the meringues in a cool oven preheated to its lowest setting, maximum 120°C (250°F) mark ½ for 45 minutes. Carefully transfer to a wire rack to cool.

4 To make the sorbet, halve the passion fruit and scoop out the flesh and seeds into a nylon sieve over a bowl, pressing with the back of a spoon to extract as much pulp as possible. Add the cold stock syrup to the passion fruit juice, then add lemon juice to taste. Place in an ice-cream maker and churn for 20 minutes, then transfer to a suitable container and place in the freezer.

5 To make the sabayon, whisk the egg yolks and sugar together in a heatproof bowl, then stand the bowl over a pan of simmering water, making sure the bowl doesn't touch the water. Whisk until thickened and pale in colour. Whisk in the cream and Bailey's liqueur; keep warm.

6 Arrange a selection of soft fruits around the outside of each heatproof serving plate. Drizzle over the sabayon sauce and place under a hot grill until light golden brown in colour – or preferably use a blow torch to 'scorch' the sabayon (see note).

7 Fill each meringue nest with passion fruit sorbet and carefully position the lid. Arrange in the centre of each plate and decorate with a sprig of mint.

Note: Using a blow torch is an advantage because it prevents the rest of the plate from becoming too hot.

Stock Syrup: Dissolve 110 g (4 oz) sugar in 300 ml (½ pint) water in a pan over a low heat. Bring to the boil and boil for 5 minutes. Allow to cool. Use as required.

Iced Pear Cream with Caramelised Pears

Iced Pear Cream:
120 g (4 oz) caster sugar
60 ml (4 tbsp) water
2 egg whites (size 1)
300 g (10 oz) Comice pears
juice of 1 lemon
150 ml (¼ pint) double cream
30 ml (2 tbsp) poire William liqueur

Caramelised Pears:
4 small firm, ripe pears
100 g (3½ oz) caster sugar
300 ml (½ pint) white wine
squeeze of lemon juice

To Serve:
sugar, for sprinkling
Triple Almond Cookies (see right)

1 To make the iced pear cream, dissolve the sugar in the water in a heavy-based pan over a low heat, then bring to the boil. Boil hard until the syrup registers 120°C (240°F) on a sugar thermometer (ie the hard ball stage). Meanwhile, whisk the egg whites in a bowl until stiff. Pour on the hot sugar syrup in a thin steady stream, beating constantly. Continue whisking until the meringue is cool and fluffy.

2 Peel and roughly chop the Comice pears. Purée in a blender or food processor to a pulp, then pass through a sieve into a bowl and stir in the lemon juice.

3 In another bowl, whip the cream with the liqueur until thick. Fold into the meringue, followed by the pear purée. Pour into lightly oiled dariole moulds or ramekins and freeze for at least 2 hours.

4 For the caramelised pears, put the sugar, wine and lemon juice in a medium pan.

Heat gently until the sugar is dissolved, then bring to the boil. Peel the pears, halve lengthwise and scoop out the cores. Immerse the pears in the syrup and simmer for about 10-15 minutes until just tender. Leave to cool in the syrup.

5 To serve, drain the pears and slice lengthwise, leaving them attached at the stalk end. Fan out the slices, sprinkle with sugar and caramelise with a blowtorch or under a preheated hot grill. Unmould an iced pear cream onto each serving plate and place a fanned caramelised pear alongside. Serve with the almond cookies.

Triple Almond Cookies

90 ml (6 tbsp) almond oil
125 g (4½ oz) butter, softened
125 g (4½ oz) caster sugar
250 g (9 oz) self-raising flour
pinch of salt
90 g (3 oz) flaked almonds
few drops of almond essence

1 In a bowl, beat the almond oil, butter, sugar, flour and salt together until smooth, then stir in the flaked almonds and essence to form a firm dough. Shape into a cylinder, about 4 cm (1½ inches) in diameter, wrap in greaseproof paper and chill in the refrigerator for 30 minutes.

2 Unwrap the dough and slice into thin rounds, about 5 mm (¼ inch) thick. Place well apart on a lightly greased baking sheet and bake in a preheated oven at 190°C (375°F) mark 5 for about 10 minutes until light golden. Leave on the baking sheet for about 5 minutes to firm up, then transfer the biscuits to a wire rack to cool.

Iced Apple Mousse with an Apple Sabayon

Mousse:
300 ml (½ pint) dry cider
130 ml (4½ fl oz) water
15 g (½ oz) sugar
dash of lemon juice
3 Granny Smith apples
3 gelatine leaves
60 ml (2 fl oz) Calvados
225 ml (7½ fl oz) double cream

Apple Sabayon:
2 egg yolks
25 g (1 oz) caster sugar
60 ml (2 fl oz) apple liqueur

To Serve:
8-12 Spiced Cookies (see right)

1 Bring the cider to the boil in a pan and reduce down to 60 ml (4 tbsp). Allow to cool.

2 Put the water, sugar and lemon juice in a pan. Peel and core the apples, then cut each one into 8 wedges. Add to the pan, cover and cook for 10 minutes until soft and fluffy. Purée in a food processor or blender, then pass through a sieve into a bowl.

3 Meanwhile, soak the gelatine leaves in a little water to cover for a few minutes, then squeeze to remove excess water. Add to the hot apple purée, stirring until melted. Add the Calvados and reduced cider and allow to cool.

4 In another bowl, lightly whip the cream, then fold into the cooled apple mixture.

5 Line 4 individual pudding moulds or ramekins with cling film and divide the apple mixture between them. Freeze for 2 hours until set.

6 To make the sabayon, using an electric hand whisk, beat the egg yolks and sugar together in a heatproof bowl until pale and creamy. Stand the bowl over a pan of simmering water and add the apple liqueur, whisking all the time, on a slow speed. Continue to whisk for 10 minutes or so until the sabayon has thickened slightly and forms soft mounds.

7 To serve, dip each mould briefly into warm water then turn out the mousse onto a serving plate. Spoon on a little of the sabayon and serve at once, accompanied by the spiced cookies.

Spiced Cookies

100 g (4 oz) butter, softened
50 g (2 oz) caster sugar
50 g (2 oz) soft light brown sugar
1 egg (size 2)
2.5 ml (½ tsp) vanilla extract
225 g (8 oz) plain flour
2.5 ml (½ tsp) baking powder
pinch of salt
2.5 ml (½ tsp) ground cinnamon
pinch of ground nutmeg
pinch of ground cloves

1 Beat the butter and sugars together in a bowl until fluffy, then beat in the egg and vanilla extract.

2 Sift the dry ingredients together and gradually add to the mixture, mixing well after each addition.

3 Place teaspoonfuls of the dough onto 2 greased baking sheets, spacing them well apart. Bake in a preheated oven at 190°C (375°F) mark 5 for 8 minutes. Transfer to a wire rack to cool.

Menus

Barry Kelley's Menu

Starter
*Salad of Red Mullet and Crayfish, served
with Warm Provençal Sauce and
Aubergine Crisps (p21)*

Main Course
*Roast Breast of Pheasant with Puy Lentils
and Chestnut Parcels (p68)*

Potato Rosti (p104)

Gratin of Celeriac and Parsnip (p95)

Dessert
*Warm Chocolate Tart with
Pistachio Ice Cream (p116)*

Ann-Marie Cheeseman's Menu

Starter
*Mussel and Butternut Squash Soup with
Toasted Pumpkin Seeds (p13)*

Main Course
*Corn-fed Chicken Breast with
Mole Sauce (p58)*

Arroz Blanco (p105)

Salsa Stacks (p88)

Dessert
*White Chocolate Torte with Orange
Caramel Sauce (p130)*

Fred Fisher's Menu

Starter
*Leek and Watercress Soup with
Mussels and Lime (p12)*

Main Course
*Pan-fried Barbary Duck Breasts on Savoy
Cabbage and Parsnip Mash with a Red Wine
and Blackberry Game Sauce (p63)*

Dessert
*Individual Lemon Bread and Butter Pudding
with a Sabayon Sauce (p109)*

Andrew Lynes' Menu

Starter
*Mushroom Risotto with a Herb Salad and
Parmesan Cracknel (p35)*

Main Course
*Smoked Haddock with a Grainy
Mustard Sauce, Potato Salad, Spinach and
Deep-fried Leeks (p56)*

Dessert
*Plum and Almond Tart with Plum Sauce
and Clotted Cream (p122)*

Susie Gibson's Menu

Starter
*Warm Salad of Wild Mushrooms and Shallots
with a Sesame Dressing (p44)*

Main Course
*Fillet of Oak-smoked Haddock with
a Herb Crust (p55)*

Julienne of Red Onion and Red Pepper (p96)

Pan-fried Potato and Celeriac Pancake (p100)

Lemon and Mustard-dressed Leaves (p90)

Dessert
*Individual Rhubarb and Ginger Crumbles
with an Orange Sauce (p113)*

Richard Shaw's Menu

Starter
Thai Prawn and Coconut Soup (p11)

Warm Tomato Bread (p11)

Main Course
*Tea-smoked Duck, Courgette Tempura,
Noodles, Baby Vegetables and a
Coriander Salsa (p64)*

Dessert
*Pear Tarte Tatin with
Lemon Thyme Ice Cream (p118)*

Barrie Watson's Menu

Starter
Salad of Sweet Pickled Apple, Watercress and
Deep-fried Goat's Cheese in a Couscous and
Walnut Crust (p45)

Main Course
Roast Saddle of Lamb served on a bed of Spinach
with a Tomato and Basil Sauce (p74)

Glazed Shallots

Potato Galette (p102)

Dessert
Individual Glazed Baked Lemon Tarts with
Lemon Curd Ice Cream (p123)

Richard Larking's Menu

Starter
Marinated Field Mushrooms with Warm
Welsh Goat's Cheese and Basil Pesto (p46)

Main Course
Sautéed Red Snapper with Vegetable Tempura,
Thai King Prawn Cake and a Ginger Soy
Sesame Dressing (p52)

Dessert
Trio of Chocolate, Pistachio and Vanilla
Crème Brûlée (p133)

Wynne Fearfield's Menu

Starter
Parsley Soup (p13)

Main Course
Boned Stuffed Chicken (p59)

Potato Purée (p102)

Buttered Cabbage (p95)

Glazed Onions (p96)

Dessert
Strawberries with Sablé Biscuits,
Orange and Lemon Syllabub,
and Raspberry Sauce (p128)

Joy Field's Menu

Starter
Grilled Goat's Cheese Salad with Roasted Plum
Tomatoes and Basil Dressing (p43)

Main Course
Monkfish and Mussels with Lemon Saffron
Sauce (p49)

Timbales of Basmati and Wild Rice
with Chives (p106)

Stir-fried Broccoli with Sesame Seeds

Dessert
Pear and Walnut Tart with
Caramel Sauce (p121)

Barry Lambert's Menu

Starter
Pan-seared Scallops on Gazpacho Salsa (p16)

Main Course
Marinated Pork on Puy Lentils with
a Truffle Sauce (p83)

Courgette Ribbons (p91)

Dessert
Hazelnut Shortbread with Raspberry Pernod
Coulis and White Chocolate Sauce (p137)

Michelle McDermott's Menu

Starter
Caramelised Onion and Roasted Red Pepper
Stack with Tomato and Basil Salsa (p40)

Main Course
Noisettes of Lamb with a Port and
Redcurrant Jus (p77)

Parsnip and Potato Rösti (p101)

Green Bean Bundles (p91)

Glazed Carrot Ribbons (p91)

Dessert
Tangy Lemon Mousse on a Lime Crème in a
Tuile Basket with Fruits (p141)

Julie Havard's Menu

Starter

Boursin, Roquefort and Walnut Tarts on a
Salad of Baby Leaves with a Bacon and
Walnut Dressing (p41)

Main Course

Thai Mixed Fish with a Hot Banana
Salsa (p48)

Buttered Noodles (p106)

Dessert

Poached Stuffed Pears on a Lace Coconut
Pancake with Chocolate Sauce (p114)

Robert Milton's Menu

Starter

Smoked Breast of Pigeon with
Hazelnut-scented Tagliatelle and a Honey
and Coriander Sauce (p30)

Main Course

Steamed Fillets of Sea Bass with
a Pernod Sauce (p52)

Fennel, Tomato and Chervil Casserole (p93)

Saffron Rice (p105)

Dessert

Chocolate and Ginger Ice Cream Pyramids with
an Orange and Passion Fruit Sauce (p142)

Pandora Cook's Menu

Starter

Monkfish and Prawn Brochettes served on a bed
of Leeks with a Saffron Sauce (p19)

Main Course

Breast of Guinea Fowl stuffed with a
Rosemary-scented Mousseline, served with a
Plum Confit (p60)

Caramelised Fennel (p94)

Potato and Spinach Galette (p99)

Dessert

Passion Fruit Chiffon on a Biscuit Base with
Mango and Strawberry Coulis (p139)

Ian Jeffery's Menu

Starter

Red Mullet with Shredded Leeks and a Saffron
Beurre Blanc (p22)

Main Course

Fillet of Lamb with a
Port and Quince Sauce (p78)

Parsnip and Carrot Cakes (p98)

Steamed Courgette Ribbons

Butter-basted Potatoes (p101)

Dessert

Baked Pears with a Caramelised Mead Syrup
and Fresh Ginger Ice Cream (p126)

Stephanie Weightman's Menu

Starter

Seared Medallions of Rock Salmon on a bed of
Shiitake Mushrooms with Potato Wafers and a
Light Truffle Vinaigrette (p24)

Main Course

Tenderloin of Pork with a Juniper and
Thyme Crust, Crispy Pork Noodles and a
Madeira Sauce (p84)

Baby Spinach

Dessert

Grand Marnier Bavarois with Candied
Clementines and Caramel Sauce (p140)

Phil Bennett's Menu

Starter

Salmon Parcels with Dill Sauce (p25)

Main Course

Breast of Duck with Lemon Grass, Coriander,
and Roast Squash (p66)

Gingered Potato and Parsnip Cakes (p101)

Spaghetti of Carrot and Courgette (p91)

Dessert

Banana Tarte Tatin with
Coconut Ice Cream (p117)

Irene Richardson's Menu

Starter
Wild Mushroom and Swede Ravioli with a Green Walnut Dressing (p36)

Main Course
Fillets of Sole with Pesto on a Sweet Pepper Ratatouille, served with a Basil and Vermouth Sauce (p50)

Dessert
Dark Chocolate Teardrops filled with a White Chocolate Mousse and an Apricot Compote, served with a Bitter Orange Sauce (p134)

Ruth Fraser's Menu

Starter
Salmon and Asparagus Pastries filled with Tomato Fondue, served with a Saffron Butter Sauce (p28)

Main Course
Loin of Rabbit wrapped in Savoy Cabbage and Schufnudeln, served with a Madeira and Wild Mushroom Jus (p73)

Puréed Turnip

Dessert
Passion Fruit Sorbet in a Meringue Basket, served with a Gratin of Summer Fruits and a Bailey's Sabayon (p146)

Myra Ibbotson's Menu

Starter
Seared Salmon on Wilted Baby Spinach with Lemon Grass Beurre Blanc (p26)

Main Course
Collops of Roe Deer Venison with Sloe Gin (p71)

Clapshot (p99)

Deep-fried Leeks (p94)

Red Cabbage with Juniper (p95)

Dessert
Iced Pear Cream with Caramelised Pears (p147)

Triple Almond Cookies (p147)

Pat Harrison's Menu

Starter
Grilled Chicken Liver Salad (p30)

Main Course
Baked Kibbeh (lamb, bulghar wheat, onion and pine nut cake) (p82)

Lebanese-style Ratatouille with Seared Vegetables (p92)

Dessert
Pistachio and Honey Rolls with Cinnamon-flavoured Greek Yogurt (p125)

Chris Chamberlain's Menu

Starter
Crab Cakes with Pineapple and Chilli Salsa (p17)

Main Course
Rack of Lamb with a Coriander and Cream Sauce (p76)

Asparagus Mousse (p90)

Potatoes Anna (p102)

Dessert
Pear and Ginger Crumble Tart with Almond Cream (p120)

Kevin Brown's Menu

Starter
Twice-baked Goat's Cheese Soufflé with a Wild Mushroom Cream Sauce (p38)

Main Course
Rosette of Lamb roasted in a Parsley and Truffle Coating, served with a Gâteau of Crushed Potato and Baby Spinach (p76)

Dessert
Rhubarb Crème Brûlée (p134)

Julie Friend's Menu

Starter
Pumpkin Soup (p10)
Rosemary and Pine Nut Bread (p10)

Main Course
Pan-fried Sea Bass with a Crisp
Potato Topping on a bed of Leeks with
a Red Pepper Sauce (p51)

Dessert
Chocolate, Almond and Hazelnut Torte with
Mascarpone Ice Cream (p132)

Susan Bray's Menu

Starter
Coronet of Dover Sole filled with Brown
Shrimps, served with a Saffron Sauce (p18)

Main Course
Pan-fried Pigeon Breasts (p72)
Pommes Mousseline with Chives (p104)
Stir-fried Red Onions with Cabbage
and Bacon (p96)

Dessert
Orange and Grand Marnier Soufflé in
Meringue served on a Chocolate Sauce (p136)

Fiona Draper's Menu

Starter
Smoked Chicken with Toasted Almonds,
Avocado and Tomato Concassé and
a Mixed Leaf Salad (p32)

Main Course
Roast Noisette of Lamb with a Cranberry and
Port Sauce, served with Cranberry and Orange
Salsa and Peppered Pecans (p78)
Spiced Sweet Potato Purée (p97)
Glazed Stir-fried Vegetables with
Herb Butter (p89)

Dessert
Rum Punch Parfait with a Medley of Tropical
Fruits and Passion Fruit Sauce (p144)
Lemon Clove Stars (p145)

Semi-final Menu

Starter
Confit of Salmon on Potato Pancake with
Anchovy Cream (p29)

Main Course
Pheasant with Madeira, Stuffed Cider Cabbage,
Lentils and Parsnip Mash (p70)

Dessert
Vanilla Sponge Pudding, served with
Kahlua Anglaise (p111)

Semi-final Menu

Starter
Grilled Vegetables with Polenta and Pesto
Dressing (p39)

Main Course
Braised Guinea Fowl with Prosciutto,
Sage and Puy Lentils (p61)
Neeps and Tatties (p99)
Buttered Savoy Cabbage

Dessert
Lemon and Lime Sponge with Lemon
Custard Sauce (p110)

Semi-final Menu

Starter
Warm Salad of Char-grilled Monkfish in a
Prosciutto Parcel with a Lemon and Rosemary
Dressing (p20)

Main Course
Seared Fillet of Salmon on Sautéed Fennel,
Spinach and New Potatoes, with Pastis (p54)

Dessert
Chocolate and Pear Sabayon Tart (p119)

Semi-final Menu

Starter
Wild Mushrooms on Parmesan Sablés with Dressed Bitter Leaves (p37)

Main Course
Pheasant Breasts with Glazed Apple Slices, served with an Apple and Thyme Sauce (p69)

Potato and Celeriac Julienne (p100)

Skirlie (p106)

Buttered Savoy Cabbage (p95)

Dessert
Bramble and Port Jelly with Lemon Cream (p138)

Langues de Chat (p138)

Semi-final Menu

Starter
Salmon and Dill Parcels with Tomato and Fennel Salsa and a Pernod Dressing (p27)

Main Course
Roast Pork with Sage and a Raspberry and Redcurrant Sauce (p85)

Oven-rösti Potatoes (p104)

Carrots and Courgettes

Dessert
Butter Pecan Pancakes with Coffee and Chocolate Sauce, and Vanilla Ice Cream (p115)

Semi-final Menu

Starter
Grilled Mussels with Pesto (p18)

Main Course
Roast Tenderloin of Pork with a Prune and Wine Sauce (p86)

Olive Oil Mashed Potato (p103)

Parsnip Crisps

Stir-fried Cabbage

Dessert
Pear and Ginger Pudding with a Brandy and Ginger Wine Sauce, served with Cardamom Custard (p108)

Semi-final Menu

Starter
Asparagus Risotto on a bed of Artichoke Hearts, with an Artichoke and Tomato Salsa (p34)

Main Course
Fish Parcels (p57)

Butter Beans and Leeks in Noilly Prat (p94)

Red Pesto Mashed Potato (p103)

Dessert
Chocolate Whiskey Cake with Amaretti Crème Fraîche (p131)

Semi-final Menu

Starter
Cream of Garlic Soup, served with a Konofa Salad Basket (p14)

Main Course
Mediterranean Vegetables stuffed with Meat and Rice, cooked in a Lemon and Mint Broth (p81)

Okra in a Tomato Sauce (p93)

Dessert
Turkish Delight Figs (p129)

Sum Sum Biscuits (p129)

Semi-final Menu

Starter
Carrot and Coriander Tart (p42)

Main Course
Poached Breast of Guinea Fowl with a Sour Cream Sauce and Wild Mushrooms (p62)

Sautéed Asparagus

Truffled Potatoes (p103)

Dessert
Iced Apple Mousse with an Apple Sabayon (p148)

Spiced Cookies (p148)

Final Menu

Starter
Grilled Red Mullet with an Aubergine and Herb Pesto Salad (p23)

Main Course
Roast Spiced Barbary Duck Breast with a Honey and Ginger Sauce (p67)
Roast Winter Vegetables (p97)
Fondant Potato

Dessert
Chocolate Saveur with Orange and Passion Fruit Sauce (p112)

Final Menu

Starter
Poached Oysters wrapped in Lettuce with a Citrus Beurre Blanc (p15)

Main Course
Fillet of lamb coated in Pesto and wrapped in Parma Ham,
served with a Tomato Sauce and Parsnip Crisps (p80)
Roasted Vegetable Salad (p88)
Sweet Potato Purée (p100)

Dessert
Tart Lemon Tart with Blackberry Sauce (p124)

Final Menu

Starter
Wild Mushroom Risotto with Rocket (p33)

Main Course
Rosemary Lamb with a Redcurrant Sauce (p75)
Potato and Parsnip Cakes (p98)
Oven-baked Baby Vegetables (p89)

Dessert
Roast Pears with Honey Ice Cream (p127)
Shortbread Biscuits (p127)

1997 MasterChef Judges

Rick Stein • Anouska Hempel • Alex Floyd • David Coulthard • Tessa Bramley
Roger Black • John Torode • Auberon Waugh • Phil Vickery • Sylvia Syms • Adam Palmer
Stefan Buczacki • Susanna Gelmetti • Graeme Garden • Jeff Bland • James Naughtie
• John Benson-Smith • John Prescott • Shaun Hill • Sir Bernard Ingham
Joyce Molyneux • Oz Clarke • Paul Rankin • Billie Whitelaw
Anton Edelmann • Lord Gowrie • Loyd Grossman

Index

Page numbers in *italic* refer
to the menus

A

almonds: chocolate, almond and
hazelnut torte, 132, *150*
triple almond cookies, 147, *153*
apples: iced apple mousse with an
apple sabayon, 148, *155*
pheasant breasts with glazed apple
slices, 69, *155*
salad of sweet pickled apple,
watercress and deep-fried goat's
cheese, 45, *151*
apricots: dark chocolate teardrops
filled with a white chocolate
mousse and an apricot compote,
134-5, *153*
arroz blanco (Mexican white rice),
105, *150*
artichokes hearts, asparagus risotto
on a bed of, 34, *155*
asparagus: asparagus mousse, 90,
153
asparagus risotto, 34, *155*
salmon and asparagus pastries, 28,
153
aubergine and herb pesto salad,
grilled red mullet with, 23, *156*

B

bananas: banana tarte tatin, 117,
152
hot banana salsa, 48, *152*
bavarois, Grand Marnier, 140-1,
152
Bennett, Phil, 152
biscuits: langues de chat, 138,
155
lemon clove stars, 145, *154*
sablé biscuits, 128, *151*
shortbread, 127, *156*
spiced cookies, 148, *155*
sum sum, 129, *155*
triple almond cookies, 147, *153*
blackberries: bramble and port jelly,
138, *155*
Boursin, Roquefort and walnut
tarts, 41, *152*
bramble and port jelly, 138, *155*
Bray, Susan, 154

bread: rosemary and pine nut bread,
10, *150*
warm tomato bread, 11, *150*
bread and butter puddings,
individual lemon, 109, *150*
Brown, Kevin, 153
bulghar wheat: baked kibbeh, 82,
153
butter beans and leeks in Noilly
Prat, 94, *155*

C

cabbage: buttered cabbage, 95, *151*
buttered Savoy cabbage, 95, *155*
loin of rabbit wrapped in Savoy
cabbage and Schufnudeln, 73,
153
pheasant with Madeira, stuffed
cider cabbage, lentils and parsnip
mash, 70-1, *154*
stir-fried red onions with cabbage
and bacon, 96, *154*
carrots: carrot and coriander tart,
42, *155*
glazed carrot ribbons, 91, *151*
parsnip and carrot cakes, 98,
152
spaghetti of carrot and courgette,
91, *152*
celeriac: gratin of celeriac and
parsnip, 95, *150*
pan-fried potato and celeriac
pancake, 100, *150*
potato and celeriac julienne, 100,
155
Chamberlain, Chris, 153
cheese: Boursin, Roquefort and
walnut tarts, 41, *152*
grilled goat's cheese salad, 43, *151*
marinated field mushrooms with
warm Welsh goat's cheese, 46,
151
salad of sweet pickled apple,
watercress and deep-fried goat's
cheese, 45, *151*
twice-baked goat's cheese soufflé,
38, *153*
Cheeseman, Ann-Marie, 150
chicken: boned stuffed chicken, 59,
151
corn-fed chicken breast with mole
sauce, 58, *150*

smoked chicken with toasted
almonds, 32, *154*
see also liver
chocolate: chocolate, almond and
hazelnut torte, 132, *150*
chocolate and ginger ice cream
pyramid, 142-3, *152*
chocolate and pear sabayon tart,
119, *154*
chocolate saveur, 112, *156*
chocolate whiskey cake, 131, *155*
dark chocolate teardrops filled with
a white chocolate mousse and an
apricot compote, 134-5, *153*
trio of chocolate, pistachio and
vanilla crème brûlée, 133, *151*
warm chocolate tart, 116, *150*
white chocolate torte, 130, *150*
clapshot, 99, *153*
clementines: Grand Marnier
bavarois with candied
clementines, 140-1, *152*
coconut: coconut ice cream, 117,
152
poached stuffed pears on a lace
coconut pancake, 114, *152*
cod: Thai mixed fish with hot
banana salsa, 48, *152*
Cook, Pandora, 152
courgettes: courgette ribbons, 91,
151
spaghetti of carrot and courgette,
91, *152*
tea-smoked duck with courgette
tempura, 64-5, *150*
crab cakes with pineapple and chilli
salsa, 17, *153*
crème brûlée: rhubarb, 134, *153*
trio of chocolate, pistachio and
vanilla, 133, *151*
custard: kahlua anglaise, 111,
154
lemon custard sauce, 110, *154*

D

Draper, Fiona, 154
duck: breast of duck with lemon
grass, coriander and roast
squash, 66, *152*
pan-fried Barbary duck breasts on
parsnip mash and Savoy
cabbage, 63-4, *150*

If you have enjoyed using this book, you may also be interested in JUNIOR MASTERCHEF 1997 (ISBN: 0 09 185322 2) which will be published by Ebury Press in August 1997, priced at £8.99